BUILD

a green

SMALL BUSINESS

Profitable Ways to Become an
ECOPRENEUR

Scott Cooney

New York   Chicago   San Francisco   Lisbon   London   Madrid
Mexico City   Milan   New Delhi   San Juan   Seoul
Singapore   Sydney   Toronto

The McGraw·Hill Companies

1 2 3 4 5 6 7 8 9 0   FGR/FGR   0 1 0 9 8

ISBN: 978-0-07-160293-8
MHID: 0-07-160293-3

McGraw-Hill books are available at special quantity discounts to use as premiums and sales promotions, or for use in corporate training programs. For more information, please write to the Director of Special Sales, Professional Publishing, McGraw-Hill, Two Penn Plaza, New York, NY 10121-2298. Or contact your local bookstore.

ENVIRONMENTAL BENEFITS STATEMENT

The pages within this book are printed on Rolland Enviro 100 paper manufactured by Cascades Fine Paper Group. It is made from 100 percent postconsumer, de-inked fiber, without chlorine. According to the manufacturer, this product saved the following resources by using Rolland Enviro 100:

Trees	Solid Waste	Water	Air Emissions	Natural Gas
43	2,701 lb	25,490 gal	5,930 lb	6,180 ft^3

To all those who are changing the world:
my love, service, respect, and admiration.

Contents

Foreword   ix

Acknowledgments   xi

Part One   So You Want to Become an Ecopreneur?   1

What Is a Green Business?   4

Finding a Green Business That's Right for You   7

Using Effective Marketing Methods for Your
Green Business   13

Remember to Be a Green Consumer!   20

Part Two   Business Ideas for Your Green Endeavor   23

Dry Cleaning Services and Laundromats   27

Eco-Laundromat   27

Alternative Dry Cleaning Service   30

Ecotourism and Related Services   35

Ecotour Operator   35

Ecotransport Rental Operation   40

Green Bed & Breakfast   43

Entertainment and Events   49

Organic Foods Caterer   49

Wedding and Event Planner   51

House and Office Services   57

Carpet and Floor Cleaning   57

Floor Installation   62

Home and Office Cleaning   65

Landscape Design   68

Lawn Mowing and Landscape Maintenance   72

Organic Garden Creation and Maintenance   76

Painting   79

Pool and Spa Cleaning and Maintenance   82

Manufacturing and Wholesale Production   87

Biodiesel Cooperative   87

Gift Basket Service   90

Organic Community-Supported Agriculture   93

Personal Services   97

Fitness Training and Diet Planning   97

Green Real Estate Brokerage   100

Green Shuttle Services   104

Organic Food Delivery Services   106

Organic Day Spa   108

Travel Planning   112

Publishing and Related Businesses   115

Environmental Freelance Writer   115

Green Product Catalog Producer   117

Publication Distribution Service   121

Retail Food and Food Services   127

Free-Range, Organic Fresh-Mex Restaurant   127

Organic Coffee Shop   130

Organic Juice and Smoothie Bar   133

Organic Pizzeria   136

Raw Food Bar   139

Sustainable Buffet-Style Restaurant   143

Vegan Café   146

Retail Nonfood Operations   151
Alternative Transportation Retail Store   151
Aveda Concept Salon   155
Bike Shop   157
Consignment Store   161
Edible and Organic "Floral" Arrangements   165
Green Building Supply Store   169
Green Product Retail Store   175
Native and Organic Plant Nursery   179
Printer Cartridge Refilling Store   182
Used-Book Exchange   186

Services to Businesses and Nonprofit Organizations   191
Fundraiser and Grant Writer   191
Independent Publicist   194
Independent Sales Representative   196
Restaurant Delivery Service   199
Specialty Advertising   202
Sustainability Consultant   204

Other Types of Green Businesses   207
Carbon Offsets   207
Environmentally Themed E-business   211
Green Venture Capitalist   214
Sustainable Remodeling and Flipping Houses   218

Appendixes   225
Appendix 1   Green Franchises and Other Team
             Opportunities   227
Appendix 2   Governmental and Other Resources for
             Small Businesses   229

Index   233

Foreword

The World Is Waiting for You

The time for arguing about whether the planet is at risk is over. Now it's time to begin the hard work of turning this crisis into an opportunity. There have been few times in history when so much change for so many people has happened so fast.

The end of the era of cheap oil has meant the painful death of the industrial revolution. It seems like the paint is peeling off the executive suites at General Motors while there's no time to paint the walls at every solar startup in Silicon Valley.

It's hard to acknowledge this historic moment as it's happening. We were unable as a society to give the industrial revolution a name for more than two generations. We didn't have the right mental frameworks for it, even though it was obvious. It was happening everywhere and you could see it in the smoky skies of London and the looms of New England. Fortunes were made during this period of change, and now we need new innovators to do it all again.

Another revolution is happening now, and we don't know what to call it. For shorthand let us call it the "sustainability revolution." This is a revolution in which there are more battles than there are revolutionaries. There is now no doubt that global warming is here. And there is also no doubt that governments across the planet are building a patchwork of legislation that will limit the amount of carbon dioxide released and raise the price of energy even further. The question is, who will grab this opportunity to create the businesses of the future?

At the dawn of the personal computer and Internet revolution, companies like Google, Yahoo!, Sun Microsystems, and Microsoft did not exist. They came later, born out of the new opportunities of the era. We are in a similar era now in terms of change, and what we need is the creation of thousands of new green small businesses. According to the Small Business Administration, small businesses account for 60 to 80 percent of the new jobs created in the United States. To create new green jobs, we need to create new small sustainable businesses. And that's where you come in.

In these moments of change and modernization, there are entrepreneurs and there are laggards. This book gives the entrepreneurs dozens of ways to seize these new opportunities and to align their work-life with the hard work of moving the planet's ecosystems toward sustainability.

If you're sitting on the sidelines, you're not in the game. This book empowers you with the tools you need to fulfill your dream of building a new business that does well by doing good. Scott demystifies the processes involved in starting up and running a new green business, and he does so in a way that makes having a green business possible for anyone with a will and a dream. There are examples of businesses that can be started on a shoestring and examples of others that are more complex. Some businesses require experience and formal education, and others have no such requirements. This book helps to fill the gap in knowledge that prevents budding entrepreneurs from starting a green, values-based business, and it also points established entrepreneurs in directions to help them green their businesses as well.

There's no doubt that someone will be creating these businesses of the future, and it might as well be you. Once more sustainable businesses exist, we, as consumers, will have even more power to vote with our dollars, supporting green businesses and helping to create a more just, equitable, and sustainable world.

Starting a business is a lot like sailing a boat. Right now there's a lot of wind blowing in this direction. And you've probably sniffed the opportunity here or you wouldn't be reading this right now. This book will help you get your sail up so you can start moving.

The world is waiting for you to get started.

Adam Werbach
Saatchi & Saatchi S
Chief Executive Officer
June 2008

Acknowledgments

Many people believe that writers live in a vacuum and that, to be efficient, it is best that they have plenty of time alone with their research and their laptop. As important as that part has been to me, it has paled in comparison to the incredible contribution made by other people chiming in, taking me under their wing, being patient with my questions, and leading by example so that I and others may follow. Without those people, this project would not have succeeded.

My primary thanks go to those ecopreneurs who contributed to this work through interviews and suggestions and who continue to inspire others through their work and passion.

In addition, in no particular order, I would like to thank Brittany Richardson, Ashley Patterson, Lisa Romney, Mike Johnson, Kirsten Gelella, Robin Wang, Rocky Anderson, Erika Brown, Shana McQueen, Ted Weinstein, Laura Klein, Ben Botkins, Dwyer McDuffee, Matt Stella, John Eicholz, Kipp Robinson, Owen Lewis, Pete Maniloff, Stacy Collett, Adam Werbach, Kelly Giard, Kristi Kleinschmit, O.C. Ferrell, Alan Covich, Dan Heffernan, Earl Blanchard, Vaughn Lazar, Holly New and my family and extended network of friends who have all supported and contributed to this work in some way.

I owe a special thanks to the management and staff of the sustainability consulting firm Saatchi & Saatchi S—and especially to Adam Werbach, who graciously wrote the Foreword to this book. Their support for this project and dedication to the green business community, creation of green jobs, and the sustainability community as a whole was instrumental in the development of this book.

PART ONE

So You Want to Become an Ecopreneur?

You *can* start a successful green business or green an existing business! It is not only possible, but it is becoming easier and easier. A wave of optimism has come over many people in the green community as a result of the increasing popularity of organic foods, biofuels, alternative transportation options, green tech, green building, energy efficiency, alternative energy, and so much more. All of these fields have created a plethora of opportunities for aspiring entrepreneurs and current small business owners looking to make a difference and also make a living. Starting a green business is an exciting prospect because you more or less have a blank canvas on which to paint your dream. Greening an existing business is also more feasible than ever, and small business owners have a wide variety of options to add sustainability to their business model.

Yet even among those inclined to hope, there is an inkling of pessimism. After all, doing the right thing, whether it be recycling or riding your bike, can take extra time and effort. And extra time and effort are the kinds of things business models don't like. However, businesses are constantly looking to eliminate wasteful spending and inefficiencies. Since *sustainability* is about making a commitment to the continuing successful life of an organization and its resources, it is one of the fastest-growing buzzwords on Wall Street.

Efficiency is a hallmark of sustainability. Even polluting industries, like coal, oil, and gas, benefit their bottom line by streamlining their use of raw materials. A company that spends $2.6 million per year on electricity in its office headquarters can potentially halve that amount with simple changes like installing high-efficiency lighting systems. Additional savings could result from installing solar electric photovoltaic systems until the company spends no money every year on electricity. What company wouldn't want to add $2.6 million to its bottom line without adjusting a single element of its actual business model?

Critics of this win-win scenario have argued that there are only so many efficiencies of this kind to be gained. They point out that some of the grander successes have actually been a function of years of ignorance and neglect of water, resource, and energy efficiencies[1] followed by sudden commitments to the chic new environmental business movement. After all, a company can reduce its electricity usage by 50 percent only so many times.

Proponents comment that what is needed is a commitment to a whole new type of economy, one that moves beyond being efficient at a company's old business model. Businesses must market green products and services if there is to be a truly sustainable economy. For example, a company that manufactures a completely closed-loop carpet (that is, a carpet made of recycled materials that can be fully recycled again after its useful life) is better than one that markets a traditional petroleum-based, nonrenewable carpet but does so efficiently. Companies of the latter type have captured headlines of late for their commitment to efficient energy and other resource utilization. The former company will be—in fact, it *must* be—the foundation of our global economy if it is to be a truly sustainable economy.

[1]Noah Walley and Bradley Whitehead, "It's Not Easy Being Green," in *Harvard Business Review on Business and the Environment*, edited by Amory Lovins, Hunter Lovins, Paul Hawken, Robert Shapiro, Forest Reinhardt, and Joan Magretta, Harvard Business School Press, Boston, 2000, pp. 85–104.

The growing economic power of the "lifestyle of health and sustainability (LOHAS) consumers"[2] has led to an explosion in the number of businesses that rely on a green business model. The LOHAS consumers tend to be very knowledgeable and will offer a variety of tips and suggestions to the green business entrepreneur.[3] Increasingly, companies are starting to listen to these high-end consumers partly because this group tends to have considerable disposable income—or maybe because companies believe it's the right thing to do. Either way, the environment wins because these consumers vote with their dollars.

Companies wishing to cater to the LOHAS consumer group may produce healthy and sustainable alternatives to products as varied as furniture, cars, and toaster ovens. They may provide a service that incorporates health and sustainability that a business-as-usual competitor simply ignores. These companies are at the leading edge of the new sustainable economy. They're out there. In fact, they're just about everywhere—in every community and across all spectrums of industries.

This book introduces green business ideas and models for new sustainable businesses as well as ideas for adding a touch of green to existing businesses. It offers you the chance to find a business you might like to run, ideas for greening your existing business, and the tools and knowledge to get going. You will find representative businesses from a variety of industries, from restaurants and coffee shops to ecotourism, from home and office services to personal services, and from traditional brick-and-mortar businesses to Web-based businesses.

Welcome to the new, greener economy! I hope you find enlightenment, enjoyment, and perhaps a new or revitalized career in the

[2]Frances Cairncross, *Costing the Earth: The Challenge for Governments, The Opportunities for Business*, Harvard Business School Press, Boston, 1992, pp. 189–211.
[3]Steven J. Bennett, *Ecopreneuring: The Complete Guide to Small Business Opportunities from the Environmental Revolution*, Wiley, New York, 1991.

pages ahead. The economy of the future will be a sustainable one. Companies will either be on the leading edge of the sustainability curve, or they risk becoming obsolete.

....

What Is a Green Business?

The all-important question underpinning my book is this: What defines a green business? With all the interest in sustainability from the business community in the last few years, the line between green businesses and traditional businesses is blurring. Wal-Mart, for example, long the target of criticism by environmental, human rights, and workers' rights groups, has significantly improved its green image. Many of its stores now carry a wide array of organic foods, offer organic cotton clothing, and have improved energy and resource use efficiency. Some stores have even been Leadership in Energy Efficiency and Design (LEED[4]) certified. It has introduced sustainability to its 1.3 million workers by inspiring employees to take on a personal sustainability project, or PSP™. The company has committed to using 100 percent renewable energy (or at least buying renewable energy credits) and eliminating waste. It only carries seafood that is certified as sustainable by the Marine Stewardship Council (MSC). It has streamlined the process for local wholesalers, meaning that Wal-Mart stores will be able to carry a lot more locally sourced goods, cutting down on transportation needs. It has increased the fuel efficiency of its truck fleet, too.

Wells Fargo, a large financial institution headquartered in San Francisco and doing business throughout the western United States,

[4]LEED certification is "a voluntary, consensus-based national rating system for developing high-performance, sustainable buildings" (www.usgbc.org). The U.S. Green Building Council (USGBC) developed this methodology as a way to standardize the measuring of a building's environmental attributes. There are several levels of LEED certification. See the U.S. Green Building Council's Web site for more information: www.usgbc.org.

has similarly made a commitment to being a good corporate citizen. Wells Fargo has greened up several of its corporate buildings for energy efficiency, saving itself from high heating and cooling costs as an added benefit. Additionally, the lender has pledged $1 billion to lending and other financing to support diverse environmental initiatives, has invested in wind farms, and has written $720 million in loans for the development of LEED certified buildings. In October 2006, Wells Fargo became the biggest corporate buyer of renewable energy credits, enough to offset 40 percent of its total usage. It also offers a section on its Web site to encourage do-it-yourselfers to go green when they remodel their homes.

So, going back to the initial question, how far must a company go to be considered a green business? The truth is that sustainability is a very difficult concept to define.

Take, for example, three "green" cleaning businesses. The first offers home and office cleaning using nontoxic products. This assurance is enough for most people to define this business as "green." The second business goes one step further, and instead of using the environmentally friendly cleansers that the first company buys from a natural food store, it uses its own homemade cleansers, which it packages into reusable kitchen spray bottles. Because these homemade products did not need to be shipped, the second business is much greener than the first business. The third green cleaner goes even further by limiting its geographic service area to one neighborhood so that the cleaning person can ride a bicycle from house to house, carrying cleaning solutions in a basket and completely eliminating the need to drive from one job to the next. Clearly all three businesses can be described as "green" even though they vary considerably on where they fall along the continuum in terms of sustainability and environmental commitment. So there is no easy answer as to what defines a green business.

For the purposes of this book, I define a green business as one that incorporates the following attributes of environmental commitment into its business plan.

First, the business incorporates principles of sustainability into each of its business decisions. Using the example of the green cleaning companies, the one constant that could be seen in all three businesses was that they first thought through their operations with environmental commitments in mind. Having this primary focus, it is safe to assume that as the businesses grow and new opportunities arise, they will be able to expand in the greenest manner that is most practical for them.

Second, the business supplies environmentally friendly products or services that replace demand for nongreen products and/or services. Take Patagonia, for example. Patagonia makes clothing and gear for outdoor adventures. It long ago signaled its commitment to environmental principles, and it was the first company to market a fleece made entirely of recycled soda bottles.

The company has a proactive recycling program to reduce its waste, and it does everything it can (within reason) to find new alternatives and innovations. The grander view, though, is that Patagonia has reduced the demand for bleached, chemically farmed cotton products and fleece materials produced directly from petrochemicals. By providing this service to its customers, it gives people an opportunity to take their money away from traditional, polluting businesses. This then creates an economic ripple that drives more farmers to organic farming and more money to recycling efforts, while sending less money to the oil industry.

Third, the business is greener than its traditional competition. An organic farm is greener than a traditional farm. A company that manufactures biodiesel fuel is greener than an oil company. Many of these cases are very clear cut. However, many are not. For example, would you define a bike shop as green? If so, are they all green? As you'll read in Part Two, it all comes down to the focus of the shop. If the shop focuses on downhill "bomber" mountain bikes, I would argue that its focus is not green. True, such shops provide hours of entertainment for customers in a relatively emission-free way, but those bikes most likely need to be driven to a mountain and then carried up the mountain by a chair lift. Conversely, the focus of the bike shop that I advocate as a green business in this book is commuting and road biking, such that the bike shop's customers can ride their bikes right from their house either to get somewhere they need to go or just to go for an emission-free ride.

Finally, the business has made an enduring commitment to environmental principles in its business operations. In the 1970s, during and following the oil embargo and associated energy crises, virtually all car commercials loudly displayed a vehicle's average fuel economy. Commercials then shifted throughout the 1980s and 1990s to highlight speed, horsepower, towing capacity, and safety attributes. Now that gasoline is expensive again, car manufacturers are once again falling over each other to brag about their vehicles' improving fuel efficiencies. Even Dodge, known for tailoring its marketing toward men who like big, powerful vehicles, in recent years has been advertising the most fuel efficient line of vehicles it has ever produced. If gas prices drop in the next few years, will these car companies continue to promote environmental responsibility? True green businesses will never compromise their environmental principles.

Many businesses will find that all or some of these attributes do not fit neatly into their business model. (Indeed, there are bound to be some businesses that simply cannot define themselves as green based on these attributes.) However, this list of attributes is a good starting point, and it will help green entrepreneurs and green customers develop their models for figuring out what kinds of businesses they should be starting and supporting.

Finding a Green Business That's Right for You

It is an exciting time to be a green entrepreneur. *Sustainability* is one of the hottest buzzwords on Wall Street, and companies from the Fortune 500 on down are taking it to heart. The Whole Foods Market recently became the first Fortune 500 business to purchase enough wind power credits to offset 100 percent of its total electricity usage. Clorox recently purchased Burt's Bees, and has introduced a line of eco-friendly cleaning solutions that has been endorsed by the Sierra Club.

On the pages in this book, you'll find a plethora of ideas for starting a green business or incorporating green techniques into your already existing business. They may all sound exciting, interesting, and new, but that doesn't necessarily mean that all of them are right for you. Instead, you'll want to choose something you can be passionate about, feel good about, and make money at.

And there are other factors to consider as well. First, let's look at what happens after the romance wears off. Let's say, for example, that you decided to start a green bed-and-breakfast inn. You bought a building and remodeled it so that it is LEED certified; it runs entirely on solar power, and it has a highly productive organic garden. You've got a steady stream of customers. You're six months into a very successful venture when you realize you don't like living in a tourist town, you're uncomfortable with meeting new people, you bristle at getting up early to cook your guests breakfast, and you are not particularly fond of sharing your home with strangers (if you did like strangers, you'd likely call them "friends you haven't met yet"). Unfortunately, these chores you've discovered you don't enjoy doing are the nuts and bolts of your business. Your wonderful green business in which you are your own boss has gone from dream to drudgery.

How did this happen? You likely fell in love with an idea without considering what its day-to-day activities would be like. Sure, you can live in a beautiful place that others come to visit. You get wonderful tax write-offs for putting in solar panels. You can take time off whenever you want. But the negatives outweigh the positives.

To avoid this problem, you have to choose your business the way you would choose a job.

Ecopreneur Rule 1

Don't forget that a green business is still a job. Run one that you'll enjoy.

Next, let's consider what happens if you pick something for which you are unqualified or completely inexperienced. You have decided that it is not the profession but the lifestyle that you are looking for. You read the chapter in this book about sustainability consulting, and you decide then and there: this is it! You work when you want, you have the potential to have a huge environmental impact, and you get paid to think. What could be better?

So you post an ad in the phone book, and you get your very first call. It's from the local university, and they are interested to know if you can help them set up a composting center outside their cafeteria, an organic garden, and a biodiesel processor for their used kitchen grease. You pause, answer with an overconfident yes, and then quickly try to figure out how long it will take you to learn all of these things. This brings us to rule 2:

Ecopreneur Rule 2

You have to know your stuff and have a solid product or service to offer at a fair price if you want to get customers and keep them happy.

Let's examine what happens when you become successful—wildly so.

You peruse this book until you find the entry dealing with a green delivery and distribution service for free publications. You happen to own an old van with a diesel engine, and you decide that this is the business for you. You set up your van with shelves, and you do a successful test run with B100 (100 percent biodiesel fuel). You offer your services to a monthly magazine covering holistic health, and you are surprised when the company signs on immediately. This is your first customer, and you're already close to breaking even. You then approach the local weekly alternative newspaper, and it hires you to do a third of its distribution. All of a sudden, you're making money. You are actually turning a profit

while saving the environment. Not only have you effectively elim-
inated two vehicles from running around town, you have created
a "publication carpool" that depends solely on biodiesel fuel. Just
when you think things couldn't get any better, you get a call from
the Locals First Directory, who heard you did a great job and did
so without using gasoline, and it wants you to take over its distribution as well. It's almost criminal: You're going to drop off publications at the exact same places as you were going before, with
a few minor exceptions, except that you're now carrying three
publications instead of one, and all three clients are paying you
handsomely.

One day you are out on your route, and a coffee shop owner
comes over to you and suggests you organize his publications for
him. Perhaps you could pay him a little rent for putting a distribution rack in his place, and then you could charge those publications for putting their publications there. Heck, you could cut a
deal if those publications let you do their distribution for them.
The coffee shop owner has just given you a gold mine of an idea.
Furthermore, he would support it wholeheartedly because it
would help him reduce clutter and make him a small additional
income. And if he supports the idea, then likely other shop owners
will too. Your business has just had a goose that lays golden eggs
fall into its lap. Yet something stops you.

Steven Bennett has labeled this unpleasant condition as the
"guilt trap" for ecopreneurs. You're doing the right thing and
making money doing it. You feel good ... for a while. Then some
day you realize that you make enough money, and you don't feel
that you should want more. This brings us to rule 3:

Ecopreneur Rule 3

Don't feel guilty about success or be afraid of profit. Embrace it.
The more successful a green business is, the more the business

community as a whole will adopt green practices. You are changing the business world in an incredibly positive way. Besides, who would know better how to spend that money than you? Expand your business, install solar panels, make a green real estate investment, provide venture capital for other green businesses—it's up to you how you spend it!

Next, let's look at what happens if you aren't honest with yourself about your capabilities. You've decided that you love the concept of "triple certified coffee." What a terrific business model. The "organic" part means that the coffee is grown without chemicals. Great. Organic is good, chemicals are bad: simple enough. The "Fair Trade" part means that the workers get a decent living wage and can adequately support their families. Fantastic. Fair Trade is a good thing—you are decidedly in favor of it. The "shade grown" part, however, is what you're most excited about. The forest remains, and the coffee is grown underneath it. It is part of a living ecosystem with monkeys and mango trees and birds galore. You like birds, and you want to support any industry that preserves their habitat while still creating jobs. Sweet! Shade grown certification rules!

So you decide to become an independent sales rep for a triple certified coffee roaster in your area. You set up a business to allow you to be hired by various wholesalers. They train you to go into coffee shops, meet with owners and managers, and sell their brand of beans. You sign on enthusiastically, hoping to see the whole town sipping a mocha latte that preserves habitat.

You set up your company's home office, complete with Internet, phone, fax machine, filing cabinet, wall clock with bird chimes on the hour, a calendar, and even a poster showing the aerial photos of a shade grown coffee finca and a conventional one. You settle into your posh office chair and pick up the phone. You freeze. Does this mean you are a telemarketer now? How did *that* happen? You've never sold a thing in your life. You don't even drink coffee! Doubts crash through your mind. What are you supposed to say? How should you dress when you meet prospects? Who in their right mind would buy anything from you? This brings us to rule 4:

Ecopreneur Rule 4

Play to your strengths and be realistic with yourself about your capabilities.

The final rule for starting and running a green business is perhaps more subtle but no less important than the first four rules. In fact, it may be the most important.

Let's say you read the entry in this book on developing a catalog of ecofriendly products, and you get excited by all the possibilities. You can sell your friend's organic homemade salsa. You can sample organic chocolates to make sure they "qualify" for your catalog.

So you get your business running, and within a year you've got a cabinet in your kitchen dedicated to recycled glass beer mugs, a pile of organic cotton T-shirts covering your futon, and a garage full of small-engine wind power generators. You're having the time of your life, and you can hardly keep up with inventory, shipping, receiving, your wholesale accounts, and your Web site when your wife says, "Honey? We need to talk…"

Ecopreneur Rule 5

Any socially responsible business includes family considerations for its owner and employees. Yours should too. Make sure your loved ones support your idea and that your lines of communication with them are wide open.

Keep these basic rules in mind when you start your green business, and your chances for success and happiness will greatly improve. Good luck, be good, and by all means, have fun!

Using Effective Marketing Methods for Your Green Business

The current popularity of sustainability has helped ecopreneurs educate the public about their businesses and the special services they offer. Most people like "feel-good" stories, and what feels better than green business these days? However, marketing remains a challenge to most ecopreneurs. Most green businesses are small, and financial resources are typically stretched fairly thin. Marketing budgets tend to get a small share of the financial pie, and the ecopreneur must decide how best to allocate them, keeping in mind that the choices he or she makes in marketing can make or break the business.

Advertising through traditional media outlets such as the Yellow Pages, TV, and radio is very expensive. Half-page or smaller ads in your local phone directory can cost thousands of dollars per month. Radio spots can run into the hundreds of dollars for 30-second ads. TV ads tend to be even more expensive. Besides paying for the media "space," business owners typically have to pay for the production of the ads as well, be it graphic design for print ads or production for TV and radio. Clearly, small advertising budgets can be quickly depleted.

If the advertisements work and work well, these costs are acceptable and should pay for themselves quickly. However, if the ads don't work, a small business can suffer serious financial consequences. One reason they may not work well is that the media outlets' audiences are too general. Though public awareness of sustainability has made great strides, it is likely that a majority of the general public may not consider environmental priorities when shopping for a product or service. Thus, marketing to this broad audience may not be the most effective use of an ecopreneur's limited marketing budget.

There are a variety of low-budget methods for advertising your business. Throughout this book in the "Finding Customers" section of each business category in Part Two, you will find a number of suggestions for spreading the good word about your business without spending too much. Suggestions are first listed briefly, after which they are explained with detailed information.

For example, in any given business category, you might find text similar to the section shown below:

Finding Customers
- Web sites
  - Facebook
  - www.WiseGrasshopper.com
- Flyers
  - Natural food stores
  - Yoga studios
- Media outlets including those for niche markets
  - Local health and environmentally themed monthly magazines
- Networking
  - Spiritual organizations

These recommendations are based on information gathered from existing ecopreneurs about what their best marketing strategies have been, and these would likely also be some of your best marketing opportunities besides word-of-mouth. So if you are interested in a particular type of business, you might refer to that business' entry in Part Two and read the parts that are listed in the "Finding Customers" section.

Location, Location, Location
The importance of location to the success of a business ranges from being vital for some (Laundromats, coffee shops) to being completely irrelevant for others (Web-based businesses). This

facet of marketing will be mentioned in only those business categories for which location is likely to be crucial.

Posting Flyers

One of the most popular, effective, and frugal ways to get your name out there is to post flyers at your local health food store. Stop by any natural food store and browse its bulletin board. You are likely to find flyers for many natural health practitioners, yoga studios, farmers' markets, and businesses that are healthy and sustainable. If you do choose to post flyers at your local health food store, tailor them to point out any health benefits of your product or service. If you are a painting contractor who uses low or no volatile organic compounds (VOCs) paints, for example, not only are your products more environmentally friendly but they are also quite a bit healthier for the building's occupants. Instead of detailing how your products are made from local and natural materials and not petrochemicals, focus more of the flyer on the health benefits of your service.

You may also want to post flyers at the offices of naturopathic physicians. This is particularly the case if you are running a business that offers a chemical-free alternative to a traditional business, like a home and/or office cleaning business that uses natural cleansers, due to the fact that many patients of naturopathic physicians are chemically sensitive. Being chemically sensitive means that fumes and off-gasses from things like bleach can literally incapacitate the patients, so they will likely be *very* interested in your business.

Yoga studios, bookstores, coffee shops, and vegetarian restaurants also frequently have bulletin boards and allow ecofriendly businesses to post their flyers and business cards. These places tend to cater to the LOHAS consumer as well, so you might get good responses from this simple activity. If you are running a clothing store that specializes in athletic gear made from bamboo, organic cotton, or other sustainable fabrics, you might want to focus your efforts on the yoga studios. If you are running an organic catering business, you might want to focus on the restaurants and coffee shops—places where people are already thinking about food.

Viral Web Marketing

Several Web sites offer a small business the opportunity to market itself for free. Craigslist (www.craigslist.com), for example, has a number of areas where you can post information about your products or services, upcoming events like store openings or sales, and the like. There are discussion forums on these Web sites that you can use to start a topic and try to generate some interest. You may also sign up for social networking sites, such as Facebook (www.Facebook.com), through which you can build a network, join "groups" or begin your own group in areas of interest to your business, and publicize your business through them. If you are coaching, giving lessons, or teaching, you might consider posting your services on WiseGrasshopper (www.WiseGrasshopper.com). WiseGrasshopper offers free memberships, and like Craigslist, it is organized locally by city. It might work for you if you run a business that lends itself well to teaching (such as a raw food bar, fitness center, or diet planning service) or giving lessons or demonstrations.

Local Networking Opportunities

Search your area for any networking groups that cater to green and healthy individuals. See if your area has a chapter of Green Drinks (www.GreenDrinks.org) or Drinking Liberally (www.DrinkingLiberally.org); both are happy hour clubs that bring in local speakers on topics of interest to their membership.

Another good idea is to browse the bulletin boards at health food stores, coffee shops, vegetarian restaurants, and other local restaurants for information about networking groups. EarthSave (www.EarthSave.org), an environmental nonprofit organization, sometimes hosts a vegan potluck dinner once per month, which would be a great opportunity to meet a lot of the local green folk. The Sierra Club (www.SierraClub.org) may have a local chapter that has hikes, potlucks, barbecues, and other social outings. Bicycling clubs tend to be more about fitness, but many of their members may well be greenies.

A word about tact: If you are networking, there is a fine line between letting people know you exist and are offering certain kinds of products and services and being overbearing and creating an uncomfortable situation. Proceed with caution, and be aware of any signs of discomfort from your new friends. Most of the time, they will be interested in your business, as long as they don't feel you are selling them something all the time.

Press Releases

A good press release may yield a great deal of free publicity. If used by a media outlet, such as a local newspaper, a press release can turn into a front page article about your business. Appearing as though it were a general interest story, consumers won't feel they are being advertised to, leaving them with a higher impression of your business. If that story also has a green bent to it, consumers whether they are green or not will appreciate your efforts for the most part, and especially so if they are green.

Patagonia, a green outdoor clothing company, for example, has had great success with press releases over the years. Yvon Chouinard, in his book *Let My People Go Surfing: The Education of a Reluctant Businessman*, wrote:

> PR companies will tell you that a favorable, independent press release is worth 3–8 times the same space paid for in an advertisement. Using a more conservative 1–1 formula, we calculated that in 1994, the year we came out with Synchilla fleece made from recycled soda bottles, we generated $5 million worth of free press for the company.

The media love a good underdog story, and green businesses, at least in the public eye, represent one of the great underdogs in society. Not only that, but it is a feel-good story when they can write about companies like Patagonia that are ingenious about their product line offerings. This combination of attributes makes readers feel positive about their world, your business, and the newspaper covering the story. It's a true win-win all the way around.

Writing and distributing a good press release takes a certain amount of know-how, but that can be learned and developed. The reward, should one be successful, is certainly worth the price of spending some time learning how to produce one, including researching it, writing it, and sending it to the appropriate agents.

The first major consideration is that bloggers, reporters, writers, production managers, and newspaper editors can be turned off to your business forever if they feel you are trying to exploit them for free advertising. This, in turn, leaves you with a conundrum because that is exactly what you are trying to do. The trick is to make the content of the press release appear to be so timely and newsworthy that someone will feel compelled to publicize it. And then, if it's a slow news day, you may well get very lucky.

Let the opening line of your press release be an attention grabber. People in the media are busy, and therefore anything that doesn't immediately grab them will most likely not succeed as you would like it to.

No matter how well you write your press release, how funny or crazy it is, or how relevant the topic, it has a good chance of never seeing the light of day. This may not be a reflection at all on your business or your writing, but it could have something to do with any number of factors that are beyond your control, or the press agent's control. The key is to keep trying. Rome wasn't built in a day, as they say, and you should not assume that your very first press release, no matter how great, will get any publicity. Don't let it get you down!

One of the most important components of a successful press release is knowing who to send it to. A great press release in the wrong hands might as well be tossed into the recycle bin before you send it. Do a bit of snooping around to find the right person at each news agency. This can include Internet searching (most newspapers will give information on their Web sites or in their pages about whom to send press releases to) or just working the phone. Don't be shy about calling; it is part of the jobs of those in the media to answer their phone and give you the information you're asking about. Address your press release to the right person, and your odds of success have just gotten much better.

Media Outlets Including Those for Niche Markets

Along with the business community's increased interest in sustainability, there has emerged a generation of media outlets that tailor their messages directly to lifestyle of health and sustainability (LOHAS) consumers. These outlets include Web sites (green Web logs, or "blogs," are briefly mentioned on page 211), monthly magazines, local green and natural health business directories, sustainability-oriented coupon books, and progressive radio stations. Co-op America (www.coopamerica.org) publishes its Green Pages, the nation's preeminent directory of green businesses nationwide. National Public Radio (NPR, www.npr.org) tends to be progressive in terms of health and the environment.

These media outlets provide opportunities for ecopreneurs to focus their marketing dollars in places where they can be relatively certain customers with a green outlook are targeted. Green business directories, for example, allow green businesses to advertise their services without having to compete directly with large, polluting companies with multi-million-dollar advertising budgets.

Many of these niche-market media outlets are nonprofit organizations, and many are businesses. Be aware that though it may seem like a good cause to support a green business directory, it is not the job of your business. You still have to make a living, which will include making the smartest decisions with your limited marketing budget. Hopefully these niche-market media outlets will provide the best advertising bang for your buck, but if they do not, do not feel guilty not advertising in them. And when you have identified promising media outlets, be sure to tailor your message to the type of media that will be broadcasting or publishing it so as to maximize the return on your investment.

Remember to Be a Green Consumer!

Odds are, you are a member of an enlightened demographic that is growing rapidly. Our demographic, that of the LOHAS consumer, can and will change the global economy and set it on a sustainable course. If you are considering starting a green business, I congratulate you for being ambitious and motivated to 'be the change you wish to see in the world.'

You also have figured out the nature of the crux of environmental problems, and instead of thinking in terms of the short term and of symptoms, you are thinking in terms of the long-term solutions and of the causes of societal ills. This is the fundamental difference between conservative and progressive thinking. Conservative thinking focuses on short-term fixes. Progressive, next-generation thinking digs deeper, to the root of problems.

Your goal to create a new green business is admirable. There will be significant work and focus required, and a crucial second-generation thought must not elude you: that is, while your own business will help plant a sapling, the forest as a whole continues to need your support. Supporting other green businesses, as part of the LOHAS demographic, both with your business expenditures and with your personal spending, will create the healthy soil and rainwater the forest as a whole needs to grow and overtake the general business community. It has been said that "a rising tide floats all ships." You and your business can and should add whatever surge you can to help raise that tide.

You will undoubtedly face a situation in which you must make a choice between spending less and using a less environmentally friendly product, and spending a bit more for the greener version. As the health of your own business may well rest on similar decisions by your clientele, it should not be a tough choice. Buying from other green businesses in your area may well be a good networking resource, a means of outreach to the buying public, and a source of potential business-to-business partnerships for you. Therefore, a few extra bucks may be a small price to pay for extra exposure. However, no one is perfect, and you also have to stay in business. You should make your spending decisions on a case-by-case basis. Eventually, your business will be so profitable that you will be able to choose all solar power, all organic food, or all biodiesel fuel. For now, find a balance that works for you, and rest assured, you're not alone.

PART TWO

Business Ideas for Your Green Endeavor

ach business entry in this book is broken down into several elements. The first element is a brief business summary. This includes a label for the type of business and a list of key points. This summary will allow you to decide whether or not this type of business is what you're looking for or if you should continue flipping through the book.

Following the summary of the entry is a "Description" section. This section gives a general overview of the business in terms of "business as usual." It is, in essence, how the business would run if environmental concerns were not at the forefront. It helps, for example, to know how a generic painting company might be run before you decide if it is worth reading how such a business would be run if it were eco-friendly. This is a generic description, and it typically outlines the basic business operations and the reasons that customers would use this type of business, and it provides a general overview of the industry.

The most exciting section of each entry is the "Green It!" section. Here you will learn various ways in which you can "green up" this particular business, and you will learn the pros and cons of making this type of business a green one. This section, without doing so explicitly, details how your business can create a little green niche for itself. For example, to get new customers, most painting businesses have to rely on their being the lowest bidder or their reputation as a dependable contractor. It's a highly competitive field, and the lowest bidder frequently gets the job—meaning that margins are slim and if something goes wrong, well, the owner of the painting business has to resort to eating his or her shirt for dinner. Those guys sometimes have to cut a lot of corners to be the lowest bidder, which may degrade the quality of the job and then the reputation of the business. In contrast, a green painter has a niche market, and therefore, he or she does not always need to compete with conventional contractors for jobs.

Following "Green It!" in most of the entries is a section called "Ecopreneurs in Action." This section relates information (suggestions, quotes, tips, funny stories) from actual green business entrepreneurs doing this kind of job. It's important to read about people who have successfully walked down the same path that you are about to take. In many instances, these ecopreneurs will inspire you by showing that you can do this, as long as you are willing to work hard and do your best. These sections are sprinkled liberally throughout the book, and they provide a breadth of examples from a variety of green businesses.

The section "Getting Started" provides the details for how to start this particular kind of business. There is information about start-up costs, special equipment you might need, and what knowledge and experience would be helpful to have in order to get going and to do so successfully. This section also details challenges inherent in this kind of industry that may not be obvious to someone new to the field. Here you will also find a brief discussion of any special education one might need to avoid certain pitfalls common to entrepreneurs in this field.

Every business needs clients, and "Finding Customers" will help you do just that. This section gives advice on what works and what doesn't, often from suggestions by green entrepreneurs themselves.

The biggest complaint many green entrepreneurs have is not knowing how (or how much) to charge for their products and services. Since their products and services are generally new and different, it is often challenging to price them. The section "How to Charge" details how to charge an adequate price for whatever kind of business you have. A great deal of input from green entrepreneurs contributed to this particular section, although pricing is by no means an exact science. A good deal of trial and error will still likely be needed in order to iron out a model that works for you, and of course, there will be substantial geographic differences as well. Prices will logically be higher for your company if you are located in New York City than they will be if you are in Topeka, Kansas.

Whether you're starting a green business from scratch or incorporating green techniques into an already existing business, helpful tips are always welcomed. And that's exactly what you'll find in the section "Other Helpful Hints and Advice." Here is where you'll get information and ideas about what kinds of questions you might want to ask your attorney or insurance agent in order to protect your business from liability and other unexpected legal problems. Keep in mind that this section is intended to offer a brief discussion of only some of the more common issues that you will want to be prepared for and that you should consult your own legal expert for your specific business.

"Team Opportunities" is a section that appears in those entries in which there are opportunities to team up with an existing business to get into that particular industry. This section gives information about any franchise or other business opportunity that you have to partner up with in order to run a business directly in that field. Typically, these companies will be able to help you get started, and they can usually provide intellectual and perhaps other capital, and they can help you with long-term marketing and strategic decisions.

Dry Cleaning Services and Laundromats

- **Eco-Laundromat**
- **Alternative Dry Cleaning Service**

Eco-Laundromat

- Open a Laundromat with a solar hot water system.
- Sell eco-friendly laundry soaps in your coin-operated vending machine.
- Invite publishers of local environmental publications to distribute their periodicals at your Laundromat for customers waiting for their laundry.

Description

Laundromats are great businesses to run in downtown areas, college towns, and beach towns, near apartment complexes, and in tourist destinations. Many people also use Laundromats for items like sleeping bags and comforters that need industrial-sized dryers or front-loading washers. There is less upkeep, maintenance, and labor involved with a Laundromat than with many other businesses. The owner typically stops by the place periodically to retrieve money from the coin-operated washing machines and dryers, stock the vending machines, and check to make sure everything is still working and that no spills or breakages have occurred. A sign on the wall asking clients to report problems with machines to a certain phone number is an effective way to keep tabs on the business as well.

Green It!

There are a variety of options for making a Laundromat more environmentally friendly. Solar hot water systems are very cost effective for a business like a Laundromat. These systems cost more up front, but with high-volume demand for hot water, they can pay for themselves within a few years. A solar photovoltaic system can also power the machines, and depending on local governmental incentives, it can be quite cost effective as well, providing years of "free" power to your business. Find the most energy- and water-efficient washing machines and dryers—with the volume you hope your business will have, these machines will pay for themselves as well.

There are also on-demand water heaters (sometimes called "tankless hot water heaters") that are tremendously more efficient than traditional heaters. Based on the size of your Laundromat and the roof space you have available, these might make a better alternative than the solar hot water system. Similarly, these systems cost more up front, but they pay for themselves quickly through efficiency.

Laundromats typically have vending machines as well, offering a variety of laundry soaps to clients. You can offer single-serving packages of environmentally friendly soap, like those made by Seventh Generation. You can also buy a vending machine that dispenses a single portion of powdered soap and thus avoid the packaging dilemma as well. This will also decrease the amount of trash that you will need to remove. If you do this, make sure you put a sign on the vending machine telling people to use a reusable plastic cup or something else under the dispenser (in case they're not paying attention and are just expecting a package—you don't want soap to spill all over the floor). This will also be cost effective because you can stock the vending machine with bulk soap, which is much cheaper than individual packages. Vending machines with food and beverages can contain organic treats, like Clif bars, juices, or organic fruit. You may also offer traditional laundry soap and junk food, but you should give customers the eco-friendly alternatives to choose from as well.

Ecopreneurs In Action

Tom Benson, owner of a solar-powered Laundromat in the suburbs of Chicago, Illinois, says his solar hot water system cost $150,000 up front, but it saves him about $25,000 annually. Benson also says that his bank did not hesitate to lend him the money since the system would make his business more cost efficient and environmentally friendly.

Getting Started

You will need a location suitable for a Laundromat, the machines themselves, and of course, a remodeler or installer who can put in the energy-efficient heating, lighting, and other electrical systems. Your start-up costs will be high, but as mentioned earlier, the ongoing costs of running the business will be substantially lower than they would be for most businesses. If you are handy, you will save yourself a great deal of money and worry by doing all the little mechanical fixes yourself, rather than calling in a contractor every time something minor goes wrong.

Finding Customers

- Location, location, location
- Flyers
  - Health food stores
  - Coffee shops
- Press releases

Typically, people seek out Laundromats, making mental notes of where they are when they pass them on the street. Most customers of Laundromats live close by, so using print or on-air advertising is usually unproductive. If your Laundromat is eco-friendly (and you should put up signs in your Laundromat educating people as to the difference between yours and others'), word will spread, and customers may prefer yours. When you have your grand opening, consider putting up flyers on residents' doors in the neighborhood announcing your opening; and don't forget to include the address and to highlight your environmental accomplishments.

How to Charge

Post prices directly on your machines. You should be able to keep your prices very close to the prices of other Laundromats for similar services.

Other Helpful Hints and Advice

People can get a finger stuck in the change slide, slip on a wet spot on your tile floor, or fall off the bench when they fall asleep. There really is no end to the potential for injuries in a public place such as this, especially when no one is watching. You should contact your insurance agent for advice on what kinds of warning signs to put up in your Laundromat and to make sure you are insured against legal action. Remember, klutzes often win in court, so it's best to be safe.

Alternative Dry Cleaning Service

• Open a cleaning service with wet cleaning, carbon dioxide cleaning, or another healthier alternative to perchloroethylene (perc).

Description

Traditional dry cleaning services use non-water-based solvents for removing dirt, stains, and debris from clothing and other materials (sleeping bags, down blankets, and so on). The most common solvent for dry cleaning services is perchloroethylene (perc). Perc is classified by the U.S. Environmental Protection Agency (EPA) as a hazardous air pollutant and a probable carcinogen. After use, it must be disposed of as hazardous waste. According to Greenpeace, noted side-effects of inhaling perc vapors include headache, nausea, fatigue, and dizziness, and in the long term, infertility in men and miscarriages in women.

Green It!

There are multiple alternatives to traditional dry cleaning. One is known as "wet cleaning." The process involves water as a solvent, biodegradable soaps, and conditioners. It works for just about any fabric, including silk, cashmere, linen, suede, and wool. The results have been mixed, though the process has been around since the mid-1990s and continues to improve. Further information can be found at www.wetcleaning.com.

Liquefied carbon dioxide is another healthy alternative to dry cleaning. There are some volatile organic compounds (VOCs) in the detergents used in the liquid carbon dioxide method, but the results are terrific in comparison with perc and wet cleaning; in fact, *Consumer Reports* ranks the results as better in terms of shrinkage, discoloration, and preservation of texture. The carbon dioxide is also typically captured from power plant emissions, meaning that it will not contribute to global warming. The draw-back to the liquid carbon dioxide method is the price tag. The system costs more (sometimes significantly more) than either the perc or the wet cleaning systems.

Other options include less toxic alternative chemicals (such as Green Earth Cleaning at www.GreenEarthCleaning.com) and hydrocarbon solvents. They are slightly better than perc, though most are still petrochemical in origin, they involve the use of chlorine and the potential creation of dioxins, and they contain higher levels of VOCs than do the liquid carbon dioxide methods.

Getting Started

A good retail location is critical to the success of any garment cleaning service. Many traditional dry cleaners are located in areas where many white-collar workers live, work, or pass by daily.

Deciding which of the above services (wet cleaning, liquid carbon dioxide, and so on) you will offer is an important decision. Each has benefits and drawbacks. If you are considering the wet cleaning method, Miele (www.miele.com) is the company that makes the industrial equipment, and you can set up an appointment or go through a seminar and/or workshop with the company to learn more about wet cleaning, the costs of the equipment, and any training you would need. If you are interested in liquid carbon dioxide cleaning, check out Cool Cleaning Technologies (www.co2olclean.com). Green Earth Cleaning systems can be researched at www.GreenEarthCleaning.com. These companies should be able to help you through the process of buying and setting up the correct equipment and being trained in its use.

This is one of the more expensive types of businesses in terms of start-up costs, but because dry cleaners are historically stable businesses, funding in the form of loans should not be hard to come by. If you are looking specifically at making the business as green as possible, the Permaculture Credit Union (www.pcuonline.org) or ShoreBank Pacific (www.eco-bank.com) are knowledgeable loan sources that might even be able to offer you some consulting services or they may be able to help you find other ecopreneurs willing to help you get started.

Finding Customers

- Location, location, location
- Flyers
  - Health food stores
  - Naturopathic physicians' offices
- Media outlets including those for niche markets
  - Local health and environmentally themed monthly magazines
  - National Public Radio
  - Coupons and coupon books

Issuing a "frequent cleaner card" (that is, a customer card that you can punch 10 times and then give the customer the eleventh cleaning for free) may help engender some customer loyalty.

How to Charge

Once you have decided on your equipment and processes, you should be able to easily calculate your expenses for cleaning particular garments. You may want to ask the company that manufactures the equipment and cleaning solutions what it recommends for your pricing, or you can spend more time and calculate your costs for operations and overhead and then set your prices according to what you'll need to charge at the volume of business you expect. In general, existing wet cleaners and liquid carbon dioxide cleaners are typically in the ballpark with the prices of traditional dry cleaners, and companies using the Green Earth Cleaning system keep their prices close as well.

Other Helpful Hints and Advice

The manufacturers of your cleaning equipment and solutions will be able to provide you with information about the risks of your business, and they can advise you on the kinds of insurance you'll need. Keep in mind that it is important to do your due diligence no matter which green option you decide to use. All of these methods are relatively new, and that is why it is critical to research your options thoroughly before deciding on a cleaning solution. And of course, make sure your company is set up to properly dispose of any potentially hazardous waste products.

Ecotourism and Related Services

• Ecotour Operator
• Ecotransport Rental Operation
• Green Bed & Breakfast

Ecotour Operator

*   Provide tourists and local residents the opportunity for wildlife viewing, adventure sports, and other nonconsumptive activities.
*   Hire knowledgeable guides (or be a guide yourself) to help people enjoy their tour.

Description

Tourist destinations usually offer a great many attractions, not just in the immediate vicinity but also in the surrounding areas. Tour operators offer transportation, guides, and support to tourists looking to take in these surrounding areas as part of their vacation. For example, an area like Puerto Vallarta in Mexico, a true tourist mecca, has wonderful beaches. It also has good scuba diving, sport fishing, the Corona brewery (yes, tours are available), rolling hills for biking the countryside, jungles for hiking, zip-line canopy tours, waterfalls, and a terrific stream network for bird watching. Most tourists see only one or two of these features unless they hire a tour operator.

Green It!

Tours can be as green as you want them to be. Good ecotourism operators observe the Leave No Trace principles. They don't disturb or feed wildlife, and many of them use alternative fuels, efficient vehicles, or electric boat motors or they simply offer walking tours.

True ecotourism operators might set up bird hikes through the riparian zone (the area on both sides of streams and other freshwater environments that is usually forested and therefore great habitat for birds and other wildlife), the estuary, and the surrounding hills. They sometimes put people on a shuttle bus and take them to a good birding area and lead them on a hike. A nice touch would be to provide binoculars and drinking water.

Some ecotour operators offer bike tours or just rent out bikes and give people maps of good routes. They often support sustainable forestry by taking people on canopy tours, which are sometimes walking tours, like those over the famed suspension bridges in Monteverde, Costa Rica, and sometimes more adventurous zipline tours or some combination of the two types of tours. Kayak tours, combined with some snorkeling, are terrific adventures that many tourists enjoy. Multiday backpacking trips are also great excursions, and they offer tourists a real chance to get "off the beaten track." All of these are more or less human-powered tours that do nothing to take away from the natural environment, and they can even enhance the clients' respect for nature. And they all sound pretty fun, don't they?

If your tour company requires transport for some tours, try to use biofuels or fuel-efficient vehicles. Electric engines are sometimes an option, as is often the case for boats cruising estuaries and mangrove swamps to observe birds and crocodiles. In some places, using alternative fuels simply may not be feasible, but a true ecotourism operator will endeavor to find a way.

Ecopreneurs in Action

Uluwehi Hopkins and Ena Sroat of Hina Adventures, in Oahu, Hawaii, started their business because they love their island and don't want to see it degraded. They felt there was a certain lack of authenticity in other ecotour operators in their area, and they decided they could do better. Over the years their business has grown steadily, and its offerings currently include not only outdoor activities like hiking, native plant education, and stargazing but also cultural activities like education on Polynesian navigation, visits to the sacred sites of ancient Hawaiian culture, and storytelling.

The company donates to all the cultural and restoration sites their tours visit, and it has a working dialogue with native groups to help on cultural and environmental projects. Hopkins advises aspiring ecopreneurs interested in running a truly green ecotourism outfit to "keep your start-up products or services as simple as possible (don't take on more than you can handle), [and] always stick to your [environmental] principles." It is hard to recover your image if you are thought to be sacrificing your principles to make a few extra dollars. Hopkins and Sroat are true ecopreneurs—they even carve hiking poles from invasive plants!

Hina Adventures can be found by visiting their Web site at www.hinaadventures.com or by calling 1-888-933-HINA.

Getting Started

You will find that a good knowledge of the area and its natural wonders is the most important experience you will need. If you're reading this entry, odds are, you have a keen interest in exploring. You can take what you know of your area, perhaps the best trips you've ever made, and research them to see if they'd make a good tour that you can package for vacationers. Set up several, and then detail them in a pamphlet that is easy to peruse and points out the highlights of the trip.

You may need a shuttle bus, some bikes, kayaks, snorkel gear, binoculars, trekking equipment, a boat, or other transport or exploring equipment depending on what kinds of tours you'd like to offer. You may also want a storefront in a touristy area where people can sign up for tours. The office will need basics like a phone and Internet access so that you can set up backcountry permits or obtain other needed licenses for tours. The storefront rent may well be your most expensive outlay, but having a storefront from which to operate may be a good investment since it would be your primary source of advertising.

Finding Customers

- Location, location, location
  - Flyers
  - Area hotels
- Media outlets including those for niche markets
  - Local health and environmentally themed monthly magazines
  - Co-op America
  - Tourist maps and publications

Make sure you have a good Web site, and allow customers to book trips through it. Many people do their research before they go on vacation, and you need to attract the attention of this group during their tour planning because you won't have much chance to interact with them once they arrive.

You will find many opportunities for cooperative marketing deals as well. For example, a restaurant may offer you free meals for your guides and drivers if you bring customers to them. You may also leverage this advantage to put up advertisements in that restaurant. Try to give referral bonuses to local hotels, and make sure the concierges have your flyers at the ready.

How to Charge

Check the competition for their rates. This will give you an idea of what tours are going for and how much tourists are willing to pay for various tours. Most operators figure out their costs and then impose minimum requirements, like "four people per tour at $95 per person." Thus, if a couple signs up but no one else does, the company is not required to take the couple out on that tour since it will cost the operator more than $190 to do the tour. You may be able to establish an effective pricing structure simply by using trial and error, but if you change prices, you will have to gather all of your old flyers and put out new ones. You can build in some pricing flexibility by including language in your flyer that makes it clear that the prices are good only through a certain date or that prices are subject to change without notice.

Other Helpful Hints and Advice

Look for places with public access, and avoid private roads, private property, and other restricted areas. Setting up a tour through private property is not a viable option unless you've made some sort of arrangement with the owner.

All clients should sign waivers in accordance with your local, state, and/or federal laws (that is, wearing helmets or life preservers). You also need to make sure you offer all the protective devices required, and instruct your guides to tell people to use them. Many times people will choose not to use them, and depending on where you are, this may or may not be the norm. However, you need to protect yourself by making sure your clients have every opportunity to use safe practices and equipment. In this type of business, it is especially important to consult an insurance agent and an attorney. Do so *after* you have planned out your tours to the last details, so that they can tell you exactly what your liabilities are and how your business should be protected.

Ecotransport Rental Operation

- Rent out bikes, electric bikes, electric scooters, electric cars, electric all-terrain vehicles (ATVs), and high-efficiency gas scooters by the hour or by the day.
- Provide maps of local hiking areas, wildlife viewing areas, or other hot spots for tourists looking for things to do and places to go.

Description

In tourist towns, especially beach towns, it is becoming increasingly popular to rent scooters, ATVs, motorbikes, and other toys for seeing the area and having fun. Typically, these vehicles are rented to tourists who may or may not have a car but are looking to have some fun and go to places nearby or just want to tool around and show off. Rentals are usually arranged by the hour or by the day.

Green It!

ATVs are notorious for being polluters and loud and for tending to tear up terrain, so better and greener options would be a significant improvement. Gas-powered motorbikes are similarly major polluters, and some scooters are as well, even though they're normally fairly fuel efficient. Thus, renting out greener transportation solutions would be an easy way to green up this business.

You could rent out bikes, electric cars, electric bikes, electric scooters, efficient gas scooters, and/or electric ATVs. If your store has green power, like a solar photovoltaic system, or if you can opt to purchase wind energy credits from your power company, you can effectively charge the vehicles overnight and rent them out during the day, thereby lowering the pollution they would otherwise generate.

Ecopreneurs in Action

Clean and Green Rentals of Key West, Florida, offers "an environmentally friendly way to see beautiful Key West," says the company. It offers four- or six-passenger electric cars that quietly carry riders around the island, as well as bicycles and fuel-efficient scooters.

Getting Started

Part of the fun of this kind of business is that you get to live in a touristy area—a beach town or some other fun locale—making money and having a good time doing so while also being green.

You will need a storefront in a location where tourists are passing by and can see your products and signs. They will naturally be drawn into the store through curiosity about your offerings, and many will inquire about places to go. You will therefore get to give people a decent amount of education, introducing them to the workings of small engines, the pollution they generate, and the ecofriendly alternatives that exist.

You won't need too much experience to run this type of operation, and what you do need you will quickly learn. Don't worry too much if you make a few mistakes, like having your equipment run out of juice. Tourists typically will rent your products based on their being able to see those products rather than based on the reputation of your business. That, of course, does not mean you should endeavor to have a poor reputation, but you need not worry about making your business run perfectly. Tourists are a forgiving bunch, for the most part, as long as they're having fun.

Start-up costs are fairly significant because you will need a showroom, a storage area, and a patch of grass or sidewalk where you can put out some vehicles during the day. You will also need a good selection of vehicles, which can cost some money up front. But the good news is that your ongoing costs of running the business—assuming your equipment functions fairly well and you can make at least minor repairs on your own—are pretty insignificant. You will need to restock inventory only as the need arises or when equipment breaks down, and neither of those situations requires immediate action.

Finding Customers

- Location, location, location
- Flyers
  - Health food stores
  - Area hotels
- Media outlets including those for niche markets
  - Co-op America
  - Tourist maps and publications

Perhaps the most effective advertising would be to put your logo directly on your rentals because the vehicles themselves will attract the attention of other tourists. In essence, people renting your vehicles become moving billboards for your store. If they appear to be having fun, other tourists will likely take notice and type your phone number into their cell phones.

How to Charge

You can set your prices according to your costs, or you can just look at what your competitors are charging and set your prices in the ballpark with them. Typically, people may pay $10 to rent a bike for an hour or $20 for a day. Electric bikes can probably get $15 per hour or $30 per day (you can make extra batteries available if someone wants to take an electric bike out for the whole day). Electric ATVs and other more expensive toys will likely bring in $20 to $30 per hour or $40 to $60 per day.

Other Helpful Hints and Advice

You should make sure people understand the dangers associated with riding your rental vehicles and advise them to wear helmets (that you provide) and other protective clothing while riding.

Some states require a motorcycle license for operators of scooters, so check with your local municipality or your state's department of motor vehicles. You will want to make clients sign a waiver of liability and hold onto their credit card or some other deposit while they're riding your rental vehicles.

There are likely insurance issues with rentals as well, and checking with an agent for local rules and regulations is your best bet.

Green Bed & Breakfast

- Provide a "green friendly" place for people to stay during their vacations.
- Use nontoxic cleaning products for housekeeping.
- Make your building energy efficient.
- Provide a list and map of local nature destinations, ecotourism operators, natural food stores, and other green businesses in the area.
- Think of efficient resource utilization, such as providing a shared kitchen, shared bathrooms, communal meals, and a communal lounge.

Description

Bed & breakfasts (B&Bs) provide a home away from home for those travelers who are perhaps looking for a setting that is more intimate than a hotel. A B&B has more charm than a hotel, it offers more privacy and amenities than a hostel offers, and it can provide travelers with the unique experience of a home away from home. Though floor plans vary, it is fairly common for a B&B to be a converted house, where part of the house has been remodeled to create a separate living space for guests. This separate living space is then rented to guests much like a hotel room. In the morning, the host typically serves a nice, home-cooked specialty. In some cases, the breakfast is as important as the bed!

Green It!

Greening a B&B is simpler than it may appear. You probably have seen the little notes in some B&Bs and/or hotel rooms that ask you to choose to conserve water, detergent, and energy by reusing your towels and bedsheets. These actions also save the B&B money, thus creating a win-win situation.

Energy-efficient appliances, suitable insulation for the local climate, an efficient heating, ventilation, and air-conditioning (HVAC) system, super-low-flow showerheads, and compact fluorescent light bulbs throughout the building will all help the business save money with little or no noticeable effect on the services offered to guests.

Adapt your landscaping to the local climatic conditions, using native plants wherever possible and limiting the amount of grass area. Xeriscaped landscaping is less expensive to maintain than lawns, in terms of both resource use (water, fertilizer, pest control) and labor costs, though it may cost a little more up front.

Your housekeeping could also use nontoxic cleansers for cleaning guest rooms. Not only is this more eco-friendly, it is healthier for the guests and workers.

Breakfasts can consist of hard-boiled free-range eggs; local, seasonal, and organic fruits; and whole wheat bread for toast. Triple certified coffee is sustainable and delicious, and organic teas add a nice touch to any breakfast layout. Opt for porcelain mugs or waxed paper cups made from recycled paper rather than Styrofoam cups.

Just as hotels and their information desks often serve as a gateway to the local community for travelers, use your interactions with your guests as an opportunity to promote as many local green businesses as possible. If there are ecotourism operators who offer day trips in your area, you should make sure their flyers are available right near the front desk. Offer a map of the local community. And there's no reason you can't demarcate a local organic vegetarian restaurant, an organic coffee shop, a green dry cleaner and Laundromat, and an electric bike and scooter rental shop. Be sure to include any nature and scenic areas and visitors' centers as well as any other green services or attractions in your area.

Your business can offer tours, bird walks, hikes, bike rides, surf lessons, and kayak lessons that help people enjoy and appreciate the beauty of the natural world, and you can make a little extra money in doing so.

The Green Hotel Association Web site (www.greenhotels.com) has good information about what a green hotel consists of. You might also want to become a member—it's good advertising!

You can also offer a fair amount of education at your business by putting up signs about all of the green facets of your building. For instance, on the wall by a prominent light switch, you can post a flyer that describes your energy-efficient lights and the energy they save.

Ecopreneurs in Action

The Greenhouse Bed & Breakfast in Kempton, Illinois, offers a unique and very green B&B experience. Owners Mark and Guia are proud to offer "homemade breakfast from our permaculture-based organic gardens, honeybees, and poultry." See www.greenhousebed.com for information.

The Inn Serendipity in Browntown, Wisconsin, utilizes a variety of energy conservation and renewable energy principles (it is 100 percent powered by renewables). It also has an organic farm and serves vegetarian breakfasts. The inn is used as a demonstration home for many green building concepts and companies, and it has a passive and active solar-heated straw bale greenhouse. See www.innserendipity.com for more information.

Getting Started

Many B&Bs are converted houses in which the owner still lives but has a physical barrier to the rental area. The B&B will need at least one separate living area (this may include a bedroom in the house you occupy) that you can rent out nightly and a communal eating area where people can gather for breakfast in the morning.

Start-up costs will likely be much higher than they would be for many other businesses. You will need to be able to renovate a home or purchase a home in a touristy location and advertise this business to prospective clients. However, you can write off any expenses for renovations against the revenues you generate, meaning that if you don't have to make money for a little while, you can take those revenues and use them directly for greening up your building.

One of the benefits to you of running a B&B is that if you want to close the place down for a few weeks and take off for the coast, just put up the No Vacancy sign and don't take any reservations on your Web site or through travel agents for a specific amount of time.

Finding Customers

- Location, location, location
- Media outlets including those for niche markets
  - Co-op America
  - Coupons and coupon books
  - Tourist maps and publications

Travel journals and the publications of your local B&B co-op, if you have one in your area, are effective outlets for advertising. It should go without saying that you will want to have a Web presence. You will also want to find and contact sustainable travel agencies, as they will work hard to promote your B&B to their clientele preferentially over the other B&Bs in your area. But realistically, a sign on the local roads or the interstates may well be your best advertising.

How to Charge

Research your competitors to see what they are charging and what amenities they offer, and consider setting your rates somewhere in that ballpark. Most hotels and B&Bs offer discounts to seniors and members of the American Automobile Association (AAA) and the Better World Club (www.betterworldclub.com).

The Better World Club (BWC) advertises itself as a green alternative to AAA, and it offers its members discounts to select hotels. Offering discounts to members of BWC will give you nice exposure in the green community, and it will help BWC spread its mission as well.

You might also consider offering a discount to members of the American Association of Retired People (AARP), as many senior citizens travel and seek out discounts through this or other groups.

Your software package for developing a business plan will likely have a calculation spreadsheet showing what percent occupancy you need to have at what rates to cover your fixed and variable costs, and to start turning a profit.

Other Helpful Hints and Advice

There will likely be zoning issues to resolve and hospitality and food or restaurant licenses to obtain. Check with your local municipality and follow the trail. Contact a lawyer and insurance agent to discuss your options.

Entertainment and Events

- **Organic Foods Caterer**
- **Wedding and Event Planner**

Organic Foods Caterer

- Prepare food and beverage services based on client demand.
- Offer healthy, organic, and locally grown food and beverages.

Description

Always been good in the kitchen? If so, a catering business can be a fun and lucrative outlet for your creative energy. Customers who hire catering businesses typically do so because they can't or don't want to create a large amount of food and deliver it to a specific place at a specific time. Whether a wedding, fundraiser, birthday party, family reunion, or just a get-together of old friends, event organizers depend on a good caterer to supply food and drinks for a gathering of people.

Another terrific potential revenue stream is to prepare packaged meals for busy customers. Caterers can do a week's worth of meals for a client to stack in the refrigerator. Busy working professionals (or just people who don't enjoy cooking) pay big bucks for good food that is ready to go when they are. It is cheaper and more convenient for them than going out to eat for three meals a day.

Green It!

Hosting an event with catered organic foods is becoming more and more chic. If an event planner wants to make a big splash with the guests, then providing healthy, fresh, and organically grown food and wine is a great way to do it. The event planners create a niche market for organic foods catering businesses.

Getting Started

The only experience you need to have is to know your way around a kitchen and to be effective at multitasking. It is helpful to have worked in a restaurant kitchen, prepping and cooking several dishes at the same time. If you want to start the business on a shoestring budget, start with smaller jobs and use your own kitchen. If you are looking to do bigger jobs, you don't necessarily need to have a commercial kitchen—you can always rent kitchen facilities from a restaurant during its off-hours, preparing all the larger items ahead of the event itself.

Catering is a business of irregular hours. You will frequently have to work late nights and weekends because that is when most events are catered. If you are renting a restaurant kitchen, keep in mind that their off-hours when you can use their facilities may be after midnight or before 11 a.m. Call around to a number of restaurants to find whether they rent out their kitchen facilities and if so, when you could use the services and how much it might cost.

Start-up costs are pretty minimal. You'll need some money for marketing the idea and for some kitchen implements, like large pots, pans, and serving trays. Organic foods and wines typically cost more than their traditional counterparts, but event planners looking to impress their guests are likely to see obvious benefits to the extra expenditures. Quality and reliability are the most important attributes people look for when hiring a caterer, so if your company has both and can also provide organic foods and wines, the extra expenditure for the healthier foods should not be an issue.

Finding Customers

- Flyers
  - Health food stores
  - Vegetarian restaurants
- Media outlets including those for niche markets
  - Local health and environmentally themed monthly magazines
  - Co-op America
  - National Public Radio

Consider strategic partnerships with local environmental non-profit organizations: you agree to cater their fundraisers at cost (meaning they pay for the food and beverages and you donate your time) in exchange for promoting your business. This can be great exposure within a wealthy segment of your target market.

How to Charge

You should charge per person, taking into account extra expenses for the number of courses and any specific requests by your client. Figure out your cost for creating those dishes by adding the cost of your ingredients to the cost of your time and the rental of a commercial kitchen, if applicable. Then add a margin of at least 30 percent to cover any unexpected events.

Other Helpful Hints and Advice

Most states and municipalities will require a food handler's permit for this type of job. Call your state government for more information. In general, if you are careful with your food, you will most likely never have a problem. Call your insurance agent to find out what kind of special insurance you may need.

....

Wedding and Event Planner

- Assist people planning big events, like weddings and reunions, by handling all the details—small and large.

- Green up the festivities by suggesting organic flower
  bouquets, green hotels, organic caterers, ecotourism outings,
  and carbon offsets for event guests.

Description

There are few people in the world who are more appreciated than
an event planner that does a great job. Large gatherings require the
organizers to pay close attention to the details that might otherwise fall off the radar and quite possibly ruin the entire event.
Think of a wedding for which someone plans all the details down
to the shape and fabric of the doilies placed under the cake plates
but forgets the "minor" detail to arrange for a "bad weather space"
Plan B. Thus, good event planners are worth their weight in gold,
according to most people who hire them.

Green It!

Greening a large event can be simple and fun. If someone gives
you a budget to work within (and usually they do), you are free to
use it as you see fit to create a great event. If the organic flowers
are too expensive for your budget but you can still host your event
at a green hotel and hire an organic foods caterer, you are still
doing much better than a traditional event planner.

Beautiful event invitations can be printed on 100 percent postconsumer recycled paper. The site can be a green hotel
(www.greenhotels.com) or a local organic farm with a gazebo for
ambiance. The farm idea is growing in popularity, and it is much
more economical than a traditional hotel or reception hall.

Music can be all acoustic (human powered), or it can be provided simply by using an MP3 player that is powered by a
rechargeable battery and plugged into the sound system at your
chosen venue. The food can be all organic or all natural, vegetarian, and local. An event planner needs to find a caterer who knows
about these concepts and/or specializes in them. Organic wine
(www.organicvintners.com) and beer are available, and local
homebrews always add a nice homey touch to big events.

Look for organic, local, and/or Fair Trade flowers, which can be purchased through a variety of outlets (try www.organicbouquet. com). Locally grown potted plants that guests can take home also go over well at weddings. These can be potted in recycled glassware or compostable pots.

You can even make the event more fun and playful with biodegradable confetti (www.ecoparti.com).

For guests coming from far away, try to arrange ecofriendly transportation such as green rental cars (www.ozocar.com). If you would like and you or the customer think it appropriate, you can even suggest that guests flying in for the event purchase a carbon offset that allows them to invest some money in renewable energy or energy efficiency projects to offset the fossil fuel usage of their travel. TerraPass offers this service through Expedia.com, with passes costing about $10 for most trips.

Some of these things may cost a bit more, but the budget is fully known and how you spend it is up to you. If you can cut a few minor costs elsewhere, you can easily shift the funds into creating a more environmentally friendly event.

Of course, you can also find all your own resources in your local area, such as organic caterers, green hotels, and retreat centers. Let them know what you are planning, and they will be more than happy to show you around, give you ideas, and let you know how much things cost. They may even send you some business!

Getting Started

Begin your planning by putting a list together. Be thorough, and let your network of friends know what you're doing. They will likely have a few ideas for you as well. Once you've got contacts with caterers, lodges, and reception centers and you have worked out many of the details like invitations, compostable cutlery, and soy candles, you will have a solid offering for clients. And each event you plan will become, theoretically, easier than the last, because you will grow in experience with each job and understand how each of your contacts works.

Another good idea is to research the wide variety of books, videos, and Web sites devoted to teaching someone how to become a successful event planner. Most of these have checklists you can use to make sure you don't forget something.

The only other thing you'll need is the ability to find green services. Web searches will help you find things like organic flowers. You'll find loads of good information about green businesses—both local and those who provide mail order services—in the Co-op America Green Pages.

Attention to detail is crucial for this kind of business. Experience planning a large event will prove helpful, but it is by no means necessary as long as you're well organized and not afraid to work hard. Start-up costs are basically nonexistent, except for the usual items like a phone, computer, business cards, and some flyers.

Finding Customers

- Media outlets including those for niche markets
  - Co-op America
- Networking
  - Spiritual organizations
- Booths
  - Home and garden shows
  - Wedding shows
  - Farmers' markets

A slew of publications and stores cater to the bride-to-be. Advertising in these publications is an easy way to cut directly to the target market you're looking for. Also consider having a booth at wedding shows, home and garden shows, and farmers' markets because these events tend to happen during your busy months (summer), and they give you a chance to interact with prospective customers and let them know how great a green event you can plan.

How to Charge

Set your fee depending on the size of the event. There are quite a few variables you can use to calculate the size of the event, but the main one will likely be the number of people expected to attend. Other variables to consider are the desired opulence of the event (country club wedding or bluegrass concert?) and the budgetary restrictions of the client (ask for an estimate of the total amount the client wishes to spend, including your fee, and then produce a plan for what you can likely do for that figure).

It's a good idea to collect some bids from event planners listed in the Yellow Pages, so that you can find out approximately how much your competitors charge for similar events.

Other Helpful Hints and Advice

Check to make sure that the caterers you choose take responsibility for the food and wine served and that the venue has insurance against any kind of accident. Your legal responsibility as a wedding and event planner should be very limited. However, you will want to make sure that all your ducks are in a row by checking with your contractors to make sure they've got the necessary protection.

It's a good idea to have a physical contract with your customers, so that you can give them an idea of what you're doing and get their approval on the basics well before the event.

You may also wish to contact several insurance agents and consult with a few attorneys about what your liabilities and insurance obligations are. These advisors can help you protect your business against a loss caused by your overlooking something important such as remembering to alert event guests about certain foods being served that have been found to trigger allergic reactions in some segments of the population.

House and Office Services

- Carpet and Floor Cleaning
- Floor Installation
- Home and Office Cleaning
- Landscape Design
- Lawn Mowing and Landscape Maintenance
- Organic Garden Creation and Maintenance
- Painting
- Pool and Spa Cleaning and Maintenance

Carpet and Floor Cleaning

- Offer specialized green services for routine and special cleaning such as treating tough stains and pet odors on floors, carpets, upholstery, and other types of surfaces.
- Offer specialized green services for cleaning and/or refinishing wood floors and paneling, tile and grout, and other surfaces.
- Use environmentally preferable cleaning solutions and cleaning and extraction technologies and tools that reduce the need for chemicals.

Description

Pick up any Yellow Pages and you'll likely see a hundred or more listings for professional carpet cleaners in just about any city. Homeowners routinely use professional carpet cleaners for pet odor and tough stain removal or just routine cleanups. Property managers typically require renters to pay for a professional cleaning after their lease is up. Businesses hire carpet cleaners to keep their retail spaces looking nice. Another reason carpet cleaning services are hired is to remove accumulated dirt that the homeowners or business owners cannot remove themselves. Some carpet cleaning businesses also offer hardwood floor refinishing, tile and grout cleaning, upholstery cleaning, and other services.

Green It!

Traditionally, this industry has been very chemical intensive. But today there are newer, more environmentally friendly cleaning solutions available. The solutions are typically odorless, and they are vegetable product based, as opposed to petrochemical based. Not only are these solutions healthier for building occupants, they are also healthier for the carpet cleaning business owner and his or her employees.

For carpets, low-moisture extraction applications are a healthier alternative to steam or hot water extraction methods (sometimes listed as "HWE" in advertisements). The low-moisture extraction devices allow for fast drying, which reduces the opportunities for mold and mildew growth and consequently the need for future cleanings (and potentially the use of petrochemicals). This fast drying is typically achieved within 1 hour, which is far more convenient for all parties and therefore gives a nice competitive edge for your carpet business.

Wood floors can be refinished with products that have low or no emissions of petrochemical off-gasses. Good alternatives are tung oil and AFM Safecoat (www.AFMSafecoat.com). Note that tung oil products such as Waterlox (www.waterlox.com) are made from renewable resources but they can contain VOCs. However, traditional oil-based polyurethane finishes continue to release VOCs for longer than tung oil products.

Little extras can help you green up your business significantly. AA Environmentally Safe Cleaning (www.aaclean.com) of

Cambridge, Massachusetts, prints its business cards on Forest Stewardship Council (FSC) certified papers, and boasts a Toyota Prius among its vehicle fleet.

Ecopreneurs in Action

Mark Dullea of Drysdale's All Natural Carpet Care (Peabody and Boston, Massachusetts) changed his traditional carpet cleaning service for a greener one after experiencing health problems. "Before I switched to a natural, odorless line of cleaning products, I frequently got headaches from the chemical cleaner I was using," he said. The key to making this a successful business, he says, is "focus, focus, focus—half-hearted efforts will result in failure or a business that underachieves its potential."

Getting Started

The job is not as simple as it looks. There are stains that simply don't come out. There are fine rugs that are extremely valuable and need special care (hand cleaning). There is usually furniture on the carpet that needs to be moved. With some careful planning and experience, though, none of those things should be a problem.

First, make sure you have a contract stipulating your limited liability for damage to expensive rugs. If a client wants you to clean an expensive rug, explain your service and make sure the client signs an agreement releasing you of any obligation for damage to the rug. Also include a clause that releases you from liability for damage to furniture. You may be able to move most furniture using "gliders" under the feet of the sofa, table, or other pieces without the need for another person's help or much lifting.

Some cleaning services charge a surcharge when they have to dis-assemble a bed or do some other heavy-lifting task.

Professional equipment vendors may train you to use their equipment, so ask if this service comes with the cost of any equip-ment you are considering. A commercial cleaner can cost any-where from $1,000 for a floor machine up to $50,000 for a higher-end HWE van. The cleaner can be mounted in a van, with as much hosing as is necessary to reach into apartments or houses. If you can, find a diesel van and use biodiesel fuel.

In this type of business, setting up the first job for a new client is a time-intensive operation. To compensate for that extra ini-tial setup time and to avoid having to reinvent the wheel each time they return to a client's home or business, most carpet cleaning companies offer to schedule the cleaning services on a regular basis. Regularly scheduled repeat clients are the goal, so do a good job each time and start to build your client list.

Finding Customers

- Flyers
  - Health food stores
  - Naturopathic physicians' offices
  - Day-care centers
- Media outlets including those for niche markets
  - Local health and environmentally themed monthly magazines
  - Co-op America
  - National Public Radio

A major advantage that you should exploit as often as possible is that no one really wants extra chemicals in their houses or businesses. All of your business cards, your ads, and your flyers should mention prominently that you use environmentally friendly cleaning and refinishing solutions. Given the choice between two companies that are similarly priced, the choice is quite easy when the consumer is educated about the differences in the use of chem-icals, even for those consumers who are not necessarily green.

How to Charge

Your business will not cost much more to run than a more traditional carpet cleaning service, so try to stay in the ballpark with their prices. You can call a few of your competitors and ask how much they charge per room or per square foot of cleaned space (many will advertise their "per room" or "per net square foot" prices in their published ads).

An alternative pricing strategy would be to offer your services at prices well above your competitors. This may lose a few jobs for you, but it may also get you the high-end clientele that are willing to pay a premium for healthier alternatives. As with organic food and nontoxic paint, many customers are already used to paying that premium for a cleaner service, and they will understand that what they are paying for is not just a commodity product. This can also help you take your time with each job and do it to the best of your ability. Commercial clients, however, tend to focus exclusively on the bottom line, and they will tend to choose the low bidder on most projects.

Other Helpful Hints and Advice

This is a pretty simple business, and it can be run as a one-person operation. Make sure your vehicle is covered for commercial use, and see the above "Getting Started" section for major issues you should cover in your contracts.

Ecopreneurs in Action

Mark Dullea of Drysdale's 1-2-3 sells a kit to help aspiring ecopreneurs start green carpet cleaning businesses. Included is all the information needed to get you started, enough cleaning products for a few jobs, and some equipment. See www.carpet-cleaning-business.com for more information, or contact Mark at markd@cybercom.net.

Floor Installation

- Install bamboo, cork, FSC certified hardwoods, and other eco-friendly flooring products.
- Use finishes that have few or no volatile organic compounds (VOCs).

Description

Floor products range from hardwoods to tiles to carpeting. Installers of flooring products specialize in the placement and fixture of floor products to a homeowner's or builder's specifications. Many times, homeowners want hardwood floors that traditionally come from virgin forests, or linoleum and other products that come from petrochemicals. Traditional hardwood floors may have a glaze or finish applied to them for aesthetic purposes or to protect the wood. This finishing solution has traditionally contained petrochemicals that leach gasses called volatile organic compounds (VOCs) that contribute to poor indoor air quality.

Green It!

Use eco-friendly flooring products. Bamboo grows extremely quickly and can be harvested sustainably. Cork floors are made from the bark of the cork tree, which means that cork can be obtained without cutting down the tree itself. Even hardwood floors that require harvesting the trees themselves can be eco-friendly if the trees are harvested sustainably. Forest Stewardship Council (FSC) certification ensures that these hardwoods are sustainably harvested.

The FSC is an independent body that certifies sustainable harvest practices in the timber industry. FSC certification means that the wood was harvested sustainably (for example, in patch cuts versus clear cuts or from young forests rather than old growth or other sensitive forest ecosystems). There is a similar organization called the Sustainable Forest Initiative (SFI). However, this organization is industry based, and thus it has a clear conflict of interest in promoting truly sustainable woods. SFI standards fall quite a bit short of FSC standards.

An alternative to traditional linoleum is Marmoleum, which is similar to linoleum but is all natural and has no petroleum products in it.

Finishes that do not contain VOCs can be used to give a shine (and protection) to wood floors. Customers are apt to be concerned about indoor air quality, making these finishes popular items.

The main disadvantage to this approach is that many of the products cost more than their conventional counterparts, though bamboo is a notable exception. The finishes themselves may also have some disadvantages in their durability and resistance to scrapes and other damages, though the products have improved significantly since they were first introduced.

Getting Started

There is no particular experience necessary for this kind of work. Ask at your local green building supply store or your local hardware store. Odds are, they will be more than happy to help you learn how to install any kind of flooring products they carry and sell you the equipment to do it.

You'll need some protective gear, such as eye protection (goggles), heavy-duty gloves, and clothing that protects your skin (and that you don't mind getting dirty—think thrift store). You'll also need a measuring tape, a utility knife, screwdrivers, and other basic tools—again, the hardware store should be able to help you outfit your business with everything it needs.

The Environmental Home Center in Seattle, Washington, offers on its Web site step-by-step instructions and tips for installing green flooring products. The best way to learn is by experience, of course, so you might want to consider getting a job for a little while with another installer as a helper, or you can simply jump in and install some Marmoleum in your own house first.

Many building supply stores deliver flooring materials to job sites, so consider that it may not be worth it when you're first starting out to buy a large vehicle for your business. If you do buy a large vehicle, however, there are several large pickup trucks available with a diesel engine, and you can check www.biodiesel.org for the availability of biodiesel fuel in your area.

Finding Customers
- Media outlets including those for niche markets
  - Local health and environmentally themed monthly magazines
- Booths
  - Home and garden shows

If you are fortunate enough to have a connection to a store specializing in environmentally sound flooring products, you can get most of your installation jobs through them. Odds are good that the store will have more customers wanting to install the store's products than contractors to do the installing. Make sure you do a good job, and this source of work can make your entire business. Also, let general contractors know you exist and are reliable, and they may well send you a lot of subcontracting jobs.

How to Charge
As most contractors do, you will bid for jobs. You should first find out what kind of floor product a person wants, and then measure out the square footage necessary to figure out your materials cost. Add a fudge factor because many times you'll have pieces of flooring left over from your having to cut it to fit around irregular architectural patterns, windows and door frames, and other objects. For time, give rough estimates of how long it will take you to do certain jobs, adding some time to the estimate just in case the job takes longer than you expect. As you become more experienced, you will have a much better feel for how long jobs take in what kinds of conditions. You might also be able to make

extra money by charging retail prices for the floor product and then getting a contractor or bulk discount through the building supply store.

Other Helpful Hints and Advice

Depending on your municipality, you may need a contractor's license to install floors. Make sure you have worker's compensation insurance as well, just in case someone gets hurt.

....

Home and Office Cleaning

- Regularly clean clients' offices or homes.
- Use nontoxic, environmentally friendly, and natural products for cleaning.

Description

Many people hire a regular (weekly, biweekly, or monthly) cleaning service to clean kitchens and bathrooms, wash windows, dust, vacuum, and mop the floors. Businesses also hire these services to clean their retail environments or restaurants during off-hours, and apartment complexes and property managers routinely use cleaning services to make a unit sparkle before the next tenants move in.

Traditional cleaning chemicals, however, leave houses with a chemical bleach smell. The chemicals that cause that smell, and the artificial fragrances that are created to mask it, can create a toxic brew of polluted indoor air. Headaches, watery eyes, allergic reactions, and respiratory tract infections are common side-effects of household chemicals.

Green It!

A host of environmentally friendly cleaning products exist on the market. The lists of ingredients on these products can be easily read (and pronounced), with names like coconut oil, grain alcohol, vinegar, and a variety of citrus products. A good place to find these products is a natural foods store, which should carry a wide variety of natural cleansers for all sorts of purposes. Read labels, compare ingredients, and ask the advice of a knowledgeable salesperson. Most product information should be fairly straightforward.

A major advantage of a home and/or office green cleaning business is that it gives you a competitive edge. The cleaning industry as a whole is highly competitive. Any competitive edge is a good one, and many homeowners will appreciate that when your service cleans their house, there is not a lingering odor of bleach. Another major advantage is that it is far healthier for you and your workers because you won't have to inhale chlorine and other chemical fumes all day. The difference in price between healthy cleaning solutions and chemical ones is negligible.

Once you have a client load, you can begin to narrow your jobs to a particular geographic area to cut down on your driving (which is a waste of time and money and creates unnecessary pollution). Sell off your client list outside this area to another ecopreneur who wants to start a green cleaning business.

Ecopreneurs in Action

Amy Batchler of Amy's Green Clean has had an overwhelming response to her business. She has a full client load and a growing waiting list. So big, in fact, is her waiting list that she is focusing more and more on her own particular neighborhood and selling leads to other ecopreneurs in other neighborhoods. This cuts down her driving, and it has allowed her to hand pick the jobs she prefers. Her goal is to accomplish all of her commuting to job sites on a bicycle that is equipped with a storage compartment for her cleaning supplies.

Getting Started

If you've ever cleaned your own kitchen and bathroom, you are qualified to begin this business. You will learn on the job, and there are few situations in which some extra elbow grease and/or cleaning something twice won't solve a particular problem. In fact, what makes the home and office cleaning business extremely competitive is that anyone with a vacuum cleaner, a few brushes, and cleansers can start a business like this. However, with your competitive edge of offering green and healthy cleaning, you should be able to quickly build a client list and make respectable money.

Finding Customers

- Flyers
  - Health food stores
  - Naturopathic physicians' offices
  - Metaphysical bookstores
- Media outlets including those for niche markets
  - Local health and environmentally themed monthly magazines

Also, go introduce yourself and your business to property management companies.

How to Charge

In general, you should charge based on the size and complexity of the job. Make sure you cover your time and the cost of your materials. Be sure to be in the ballpark with your competitors on price. However, you do offer a healthier and better service, so don't worry if you can't beat their price.

Other Helpful Hints and Advice

Homeowners that hire these services may choose to trust you with a key to their house. If they do so, be careful not to move any valuables because homeowners might get nervous and accuse you of theft. Be courteous and kind when speaking with clients. Trust is a huge issue once you enter a home, and if you earn that trust, the client will likely stay with you.

....

Landscape Design

- Design a landscape that incorporates trees, shrubs, and other plants that thrive in your local climate and subsequently will need less maintenance, fertilizer, and water than plants that are native to other places.
- Increase a building's energy efficiency with shade trees and trees that decrease heat loss from winter winds.
- Plan edible landscapes that can provide fruit, vegetables, and herbs to a homeowner.

Description

Landscaping can add great value to a home's resale value, as well as provide useful areas for people and pets. Planning a landscape can be a great deal of fun, but it also requires a great deal of work. Most homeowners don't know enough or don't have time to plan their landscaping.

A landscape designer will draw up a plan for a landscape (new or renovation) and present it to a homeowner. All the actual work of digging, planting, laying sod, and so on, can be outsourced to a landscaping company with the heavy equipment needed, or you can do it yourself if you want to invest a bit more in a vehicle and equipment.

Green It!

Use native vegetation as appropriate for local climatic conditions. Native plants will require less watering, fertilizing, pest control, and other environmentally taxing maintenance. Locally owned greenhouses or nurseries will likely have a wide array of native plants. Ask the knowledgeable garden experts for advice on native plants if you have any questions.

Xeriscape designs reduce or eliminate the amount of grass and/or turf in a particular landscape and replace it with mulch, compost, a ground cover like English ivy, or some other attractive material. This substitution greatly reduces the amount of watering, fertilizing, and maintenance. If you want to use some turf (grass) areas, consider rhizomatous tall fescue (RTF), buffalo grass, or some native grass as opposed to the traditional Kentucky bluegrass used across the country for its rich green color. If you are unsure of what grows best where, seek the advice of an agent in the state extension service in your state's agricultural department or a garden expert at your local nursery.

You can also plant trees according to environmental principles. Deciduous trees can shade the house in the summer and warm it in the winter when they lose their leaves. Coniferous trees can help shield the house from freezing winds in the winter.

Another great opportunity for landscape designers is to create edible landscapes. Fruit trees, berry bushes, vegetables, and herb gardens can all be fun additions to a landscape. Growing food on site not only eliminates the need to transport agricultural products but also provides a terrific experience for children to learn about where their food comes from.

Getting Started

A formal education in landscape design (many universities offer landscape design as a major) is helpful but not entirely necessary. You might simply consider apprenticing for another landscape planner first. If you choose to work for someone else before striking off on your own, the business you work for need not be green for you to learn how to do the job.

Communicate well with your customers about what they'll be getting and when, and make sure the job gets done right. It may sound like a no-brainer, but be 100 percent certain that you ask what kinds of plants and landscape the clients want. They may want a landscape that requires little maintenance, or they may have other very specific desires. Either way, find out as much as you can from them about what they want and need, and then hit the drawing boards and return with a diagram and outline of your landscape design. When you present the design, show your clients actual sample materials of any mulch, bark chip, or rocks you'll be putting down. Showing sample materials to your clients is especially important if you are also the person who will be implementing the design—you will be covered if they complain about the color of the mulch after the job's been done.

Start-up costs for this business are negligible. All you need is knowledge, some graph paper, a tape measure, and a pencil. You might need to start by doing a job in your own yard. Once you have a finished landscape, you can then use it as a model of what you can do and show pictures of it to others. If you can get your own yard included on a home and garden tour, especially a green home and garden tour, it will be terrific exposure for you.

A key element is to find a reliable company to do the manual labor unless you want to do it yourself. You might have to try a few before finding someone you like.

Finding Customers
- Web
  - www.WiseGrasshopper.com
- Media outlets including those for niche markets
  - Local health and environmentally themed monthly magazines
- Booths
  - Home and garden shows
- Press releases

Another fun way to advertise this type of business is to leave a sign in the yards of the people whose landscapes you've designed. Frequently, if they're pleased with your work, customers will be happy to have a sign in their yard that says, "Ecofriendly landscape design by Earthen Landscapes, Inc. Free Consultation, 555-2121." You might also offer customers a month's free landscape maintenance for the privilege of using their yards to advertise your service.

How to Charge

This is a great business in terms of how to charge and how much to charge. After you talk to a potential client about what you may do, design three different landscapes for the client to choose from. Take these designs to several landscape contractors and ask them to bid the job for you. Make sure your diagram is accurate with dimensions, obstacles and other challenges, and make sure you have an idea of how compacted the soil is (how hard the job will be).

Once you have a couple of bids for each design, mark the over-all price up significantly enough to cover your own time and to give you a little cushion should anything go wrong. Then bring these numbers and designs to your client and have him or her choose one. Explain that half the money will be due up front and half will be due at the completion of the project. If pressed, explain that this amount is necessary for you to buy the plants, soil, compost, mulch, rocks, and other materials for the job. Then you can subcontract the work for the job to your contractor, and you can oversee the process. You may also choose to simply sell the design to the customer, and leave them to find contractors fit for the job. This should be arranged between you and the customer.

Other Helpful Hints and Advice

Be wary of borders. Don't plant trees right on a property line, for example. Consider sidewalks as well because tree roots might lift up or break concrete segments. If you subcontract out the physical labor, make sure you oversee the job to see that it's done right, and get a contract from your subcontractor guaranteeing the work for at least 90 days. This should give you enough time to document any shortcomings and to see if the more expensive plants survive.

••

Lawn Mowing and Landscape Maintenance

- Maintain lawns and landscapes through mowing, trimming, edging, sweeping, hedge trimming, and leaf raking using nonpolluting equipment.
- Use a vehicle that gets good gas mileage and/or one that can use a biofuel.

Description

Home and office landscapes require regular maintenance to keep them looking good. Usually, this means weekly mowing, trimming, edging, cleanup, and hedge trimming. Traditionally, this type of work has been done with unregulated, two-stroke lawn mowers, weed whackers, and other equipment powered by a gas and oil mixture that is very polluting. The emissions of these kinds of equipment include benzene, butadiene and other known or suspected carcinogens, as well as carbon monoxide and other compounds that contribute to ground-level ozone and smog formation.

According to the U.S. Environmental Protection Agency (EPA), running a traditional mower for one hour can create an amount of volatile organic compound (VOC—a family of chemicals including many known and suspected carcinogens) pollution equivalent to that of driving a car 650 miles! In addition, most lawn care companies operate at least one heavy-duty truck that does not have to meet the same emission standards as a car and that may get as little as 6 to 10 miles per gallon.

Green It!

Nonpolluting lawn equipment includes electric- and manual-powered implements. Classic push-reel mowers, if kept sharp, are versatile and durable enough to cut as many lawns as the person pushing them is capable of. Several companies, including

Black & Decker, make battery-powered electric mowers capable of mowing several small lawns per day. There are also entire lines of weed whackers, edgers, and hard-surface sweepers that use interchangeable and rechargeable batteries. For harder jobs, you can use a corded electric mower. All of this equipment generates drastically less pollution than traditional lawn care equipment. Electric hedge trimmers round out your equipment needs, and they will perform well with most small to medium-sized branches.

There are several advantages a green landscape maintenance company has over a business-as-usual competitor. First, efficiency means cost savings. Small cars or trucks, electric mowers and other eco-friendly tools often cost quite a bit less to operate than their counterparts. Second, smaller yards are a perfect niche for this kind of business. Bigger lawn care operations, with their giant riding mowers, can't really get in and out of small yards. Thus, you can spend 5 to 10 minutes mowing a small lawn whereas a bigger lawn care company would need a greater amount of time and effort to manage their too-large equipment. Third, smaller mowers don't break sprinkler heads nearly as often as those big riding mowers.

There are disadvantages as well. There will be times when the grass is sopping wet, or a client has waited until he or she has a jungle before calling you, and in those cases, electric mowers just won't cut it (literally). Just be up front with clients and let them know that there are limits to what you can do. The majority of the time, the electric or push-reel mowers work as well or better.

Ecopreneurs In Action

Kelly Giard of Clean Air Lawn Care says the biggest obstacle his company has faced is getting customers to believe that his company's service is comparable to a traditional competitor. "We just showed them that it was, let them test it out, not sign contracts, that sort of thing." Giard advises aspiring ecopreneurs to "keep the focus on the green side; don't get caught up in the money, which will take care of itself if you do a good enough job." Marketing has been pretty easy for Giard. He says, "The key people in the environmental community all kind of know each other, and you just have to get into that circle.... The first year you expose people to the idea; the second year you start to see them track you down."

See www.CleanAirLawnCare.com for more information.

Getting Started

While there is no particular type of experience that is absolutely necessary to start an eco-friendly lawn care business, some land-scaping and landscape maintenance experience would go a long way to helping you avoid many common pitfalls.

You will need to spend between $5,000 and $20,000 on equip-ment (not including a vehicle), and you will need a place to store your equipment and charge any related batteries overnight. You'll need a couple of lawn mowers, two to three weed whackers, two blowers, and about 25 interchangeable batteries. (Black & Decker's batteries work for their weed whackers, hedgers, and blowers interchangeably—just make sure you buy the ones that take the same size batteries.) You will also need a couple of appropriate extension cords (with sufficient amperage for an electric mower, should you buy a corded one), a utility trailer, and a vehicle with a hitch.

You'll need a vehicle capable of towing a small trailer (most vehicles have this capability: the vehicle owner's manual will say what its towing capacity is, and anything that can tow up to 1,000 pounds will be more than adequate). A car or light truck that uses diesel gas can also utilize biodiesel fuel (check to see if biodiesel is available in your community at www.biodiesel.org). Other than that, some heavy-duty gloves, a wheelbarrow, a collapsible ladder, hearing and vision protection, and you're ready to go.

This business, in most locales, is seasonal. Thus, make sure you have enough money to get through the winter, or be prepared to work a different job during the off season.

Finding Customers

- Flyers
  - ○ Door-to-door in certain neighborhoods
- Media outlets including those for niche markets
  - ○ Local health and environmentally themed monthly magazines
  - ○ National Public Radio
- Booths
  - ○ Home and garden shows
- Press releases

Remember that since this business is seasonal in most locales, a media blitz at the appropriate time is likely to be much more effective than annual and/or continuous advertising.

How to Charge

Bidding a job should incorporate a number of considerations. In general, the bigger the lawn, the bigger the bid should be. However, the breadth of service requested by your client should also enter the equation (that is, gates, pets, and tricky or complex landscaping). If your client wants you to maintain flower beds by pulling weeds, replacing mulch or compost, and clipping dead flower heads, you should charge an extra fee to cover the time required to perform those tasks as well.

Other Helpful Hints and Advice

Though rare, injuries using electric- or manual-powered types of power tools can still be extremely painful and debilitating. Make sure your employees have adequate protection. This may include hard hats and heavy-duty gloves. Liability and worker's compensation insurance are the basic essentials for this kind of work. Many customers may also want tree-trimming services. This requires a good deal of extra equipment and expertise, and it opens up extra liability. It is advisable to outsource these jobs to ISA certified arborists while you are getting started.

Team Opportunities
Clean Air Lawn Care of Fort Collins, Colorado, is expanding rapidly across all 50 states. Franchise opportunities may be available. See www.CleanAirLawnCare.com or call 1-888-969-3669 for more information.

Organic Garden Creation and Maintenance

- Help homeowners create organic gardens with produce of their choosing.
- Provide basic weekly maintenance services, including weeding and adding organic fertilizations and other soil amenities and performing drip system irrigation maintenance.

Description
Gardening companies maintain flower beds, pull weeds, remove dead flowers, and plant a variety of plants to keep the place colorful and beautiful throughout the year. They also install and maintain irrigation systems (sprinklers or drip systems).

Green It!
Many homeowners want to have a steady supply of organic veggies from their own garden, but, either they don't want to do their own gardening, they don't know how to do it, or they don't have time.

You can work with existing landscapes, clearing land of grass or weeds, and begin organic gardens for people. You can use certain amenities for the soil, such as certified organic fertilizers, mulch, compost, and earthworms. Then you plant tomatoes, corn, sunflowers, carrots, peppers, squash, and any other plants your clients want, making sure to give the plants adequate space to grow throughout the growing season (seed packets and live plants should come with labels for how much space, water, and so on the plants will need).

Set up a drip system to water those specific plants. This type of system will require less water usage than a sprinkler system, and it will reduce the amount of weeds that are able to recolonize and thrive in the garden.

Weekly maintenance follows. You set up a program to come to the home once a week, spending as much time on each visit as needed to maintain the garden. You will need to pull weeds and keep an eye on the health of the plants so that you can address any water, shade, competition, or other issues that should arise.

Getting Started

This is a terrific business for avid gardeners, and an easy one to run on your own. It gives you the opportunity to set your own schedule and work outdoors, with your hands in the dirt, as they say. You will need to know your way around a garden and not mind getting your hands dirty. Knowledge of basic organic gardening principles will also help you answer clients' questions, as well as foresee and prevent many of the common problems in a garden.

Many garden centers deliver large quantities of compost, mulch, and other soil amenities, as well as trees, shrubs, and other plants. However, having your own vehicle that can handle wheelbarrows, 50-pound bags of compost, organic fertilizer, and rows of seedlings (in other words, a vehicle you don't mind getting a bit dirty) may be necessary for your business.

Getting trained in the installation of drip irrigation systems is as simple as going to the local garden store that sells them and asking for a bit of instruction. You can always outsource more complex irrigation systems to irrigation companies (provide a good diagram of what you want, then get bids from several contractors in the Yellow Pages).

This is a business you can begin on a shoestring. For information on ecofriendly tools you might need, visit www.CleanAirGardening.com.

Finding Customers

- Flyers
    - Health food stores
    - Door-to-door in certain neighborhoods
    - Vegetarian restaurants
- Media outlets including those for niche markets
    - Local health and environmentally themed monthly magazines
- Booths
    - Home and garden shows

Business partnerships are usually very lucrative for both partners, so make sure you find out if there are any prospective partners in your area such as natural lawn care companies, ecofriendly lawn maintenance companies, or landscape architects that specialize in native or edible landscapes. Buy these people a cup of coffee and let the networking begin.

How to Charge

You will charge a larger amount for setting up the garden, and a smaller, regular amount for the weekly maintenance. You can bundle the services and offer a discount if customers sign on for both. What you charge will be the combination of all the costs of the plants, the fertilizers and other soil amenities that you use, and the labor in terms of the number of hours you think it will take you to complete the job. If you don't have experience in this regard, don't worry too much about it. Just give the best bid you can, and then modify it in future jobs. You might start at $25 to $30 per hour, which you can then adapt as necessary.

Other Helpful Hints and Advice

You will need to have insurance on any vehicle you use. Also, be sure to talk to the homeowners to let them know what it is you'll be doing because there may be some concerns about allergies. If asked, show people samples of your products or their labels because this will reassure them that what you're doing is a healthy alternative to the more common chemical-based services.

. . . .

Painting

- Apply natural paints and plasters that are free of volatile organic compounds (VOCs).

Description

Painting jobs range in size and complexity from putting up a fresh coat of paint in a child's bedroom to redoing the entire interior of a house. Exterior jobs (siding, decks, patio, and trims) are more involved and usually require more elaborate and specialized equipment such as extension ladders and power sprayer applicators.

People hire painting contractors for a variety of reasons. First, they may not *want* to do the job themselves. It's a dirty job, and it is time-consuming. Second, they may be scared of staining a carpet or some furniture. Third, they may not have the ladders, sprayers, or some of the other specialized equipment needed for tougher jobs.

Traditional paints contain a variety of volatile organic compounds. Most people keep the windows open the day or two after painting, so that the fumes from the drying paint don't make people sick. However, paint continues to "off-gas" into the indoor air environment throughout the life of the paint, albeit in smaller quantities than when it was first applied. These VOCs have conclusively been linked to higher rates of asthma, and they are implicated as hormone disruptors and known or suspected carcinogens. Headaches, allergic reactions, and respiratory tract infections may also result from chronic exposures to VOCs.

Green It!

Healthier paints with low and no VOCs are made from mostly all-natural ingredients. The advantages of these kinds of paints are clear. They're more eco-friendly and healthier for the building occupants and the workers applying them. However, they do tend to cost more than generic paints, and some have different application requirements. Be sure to follow instructions explicitly.

One of the other major advantages of using all-natural paints is that customers who hire painting contractors typically call several of them and get competing bids, usually taking the lowest bidder. If you were a generic painting contractor, this would mean that you would virtually always have to compete on price, resulting in very slim profit margins. Green painting contractors offer a different service. Many customers with chemical sensitivities can't hire generic contractors, and many others would prefer your services even if the price were higher.

Getting Started

Learning to paint like a pro is not necessarily easy, but there are many resources you can use to gain the knowledge and experience you need. You could start by working for a painting company as an assistant for a job or two. Also, local home improvement centers, eager to earn contractors' business, can guide you through the process. You will learn how to protect floors, furniture, window frames, ceilings, and other surfaces you wish to keep clean. You will learn about primers, sealants, and plasters, as well as types of brush strokes to accomplish a certain look or feel. Manufacturers of sprayers and other equipment will also provide assistance, and you will find a plethora of information on their Web sites.

Expenses up front will include a couple of ladders, uniforms for you and your crew, and painting equipment including trays, painter's masking tape, rollers, some good-quality brushes, mixers, and furniture and carpet protectors such as tarps and plastic sheets. You will also want to get breathing masks and eye protection. The breathing masks are important not as much for the new paint you'll be putting up but more for the old paint you may be required to take down and the holes in the walls you'll have to seal that are full of dust.

You will also need a van or other vehicle big enough to carry all of your equipment. As a suggestion, Sprinter vans would be a great option. They have tons of storage space and reasonable gas mileage (25 to 28 miles per gallon); and the diesel Sprinter vans can use biodiesel fuel.

Finding Customers
- Flyers
  - Health food stores
  - Naturopathic physicians' offices
- Media outlets including those for niche markets
  - Local health and environmentally themed monthly magazines
- Booths
  - Home and garden shows

How to Charge
Bid on the job. You can charge by the room or by the hour. Build in a margin sufficiently high that if something goes wrong, you won't go belly up fixing it. In general, each job should pay for the paints, plasters, sealants, and so on that you use, in addition to paying for labor and an extra margin for your fixed costs such as your ladder, plastic sheets, or van.

Other Helpful Hints and Advice
You will need to have contracts with your clients. Once they have accepted your bid, make them pay half the cost up front, with the balance due upon completion of the work. In the contract, make sure you stipulate what possible unexpected damages you will and will not be responsible for.

Pool and Spa Cleaning and Maintenance

- Provide nonchemical alternatives for keeping pools and spas clean.
- Perform regular cleaning and maintenance of pools and spas.
- Keep the alternative filter systems running smoothly.

Description

People with swimming pools or spas typically use chlorine-based chemicals to kill mold, algae and bacteria. Busy people hire pool and spa services to deliver and perhaps administer these chemicals on a regular basis, as well as vacuuming the pools, cleaning filters, and so on.

The amount of chemicals used in the pool and spa industry is somewhat mind-boggling. There are roughly 6.2 million hot tubs in the United States, and according to information posted on the Web site www.AhhNatural.com, if they were all switched to a non-toxic maintenance alternative, it could save 20 billion tons of chemical-laden wastewater from entering the ecosystem annually.

Green It!

Healthier alternatives abound. Search for non-chemical or reduced chemical alternatives available in your area. These may include ozonators, ultraviolet sanitizers, mineral sanitizers, ionizers, and salt chlorine generators. Ozonators generate ozone (a byproduct of oxygen decomposition), which can kill bacteria and algae. Ozonators typically run in conjunction with the filter pump, so that water passing by the filter will get sterilized by the ozonator. However, when the pump is off, algae and bacteria, especially in crevices and slow moving sections of the pool, are free to continue growing. Thus, most retailers suggest a complementary sanitizer in addition to the ozonator, such as chlorine. Ozonators, then, reduce the overall load of chlorine used in a pool or spa, but are not typically sufficient by themselves to keep a pool clean. Chlorine, Bromine, ionization or mineral sanitizers can be used in conjunction with the ozonator to complete the job. Ultraviolet sanitizers kill most bacteria and algae coming back into the circulatory system, providing perhaps the best alternative water sanitizer available. They do not eliminate all bacteria, and do not break down organic waste (dead skin cells, hair, etc.), and thus may require a complementary treatment as well. Hydrogen peroxide may be the best complementary solution to both ozonators and UV sanitizers. Hydrogen peroxide, commonly used to clean cuts, is a very nontoxic additive that kills bacteria, algae, and helps break down organic material. Hydrogen peroxide used in the home is very dilute, whereas the industrial stuff made for pools and spas is much more concentrated. It can be irritating to skin, so it should be used when no one is in the pool or spa. It breaks down naturally to two byproducts: pure water and pure oxygen. Thus, within a few minutes of adding it to a pool or spa, there is little or no remnant of the solution. You can also become a distributor/salesman for natural hot tub treatments, such as those offered by ahhnatural.com, a non-toxic hot tub maintenance company (www.ahhnatural.com), and use these treatments in conjunction with one or more of the other alternatives above, or simply offer them by themselves.

Find pool retailers who carry these alternatives and go talk to the owners or managers of these businesses. You'll find they will be most helpful to you, as they are always interested in helping contractors get started... if you're happier with their products, you'll end up buying more from them.

Getting Started

You can learn most of what you need to from retailers who carry non-chemical alternative sanitizers and from the Web sites affiliated with those products (manufacturers' Web sites). You'll need a way to get from house to house, a professional looking uniform, and some general pool and spa cleaning equipment, like vacuums, hoses, and scrub brushes. Give clients a flyer with all their alternatives in it, including the prices involved, and allow them to choose which treatment option they would prefer.

Pools with large deciduous trees nearby may need more regular cleaning (due to falling leaves). Also ask your retailer for an education about heated pools, as they present a slew of challenges of their own. This business, in most locales, is seasonal. Thus, make sure you have enough money to get through the winter, or be prepared to work a different job in the wintertime.

Finding Customers

- Flyers
  - ○ Health food stores
  - ○ Door-to-door in certain neighborhoods
  - ○ Naturopathic physicians' offices
- Booths
  - ○ Home and garden shows

It shouldn't be too difficult to find the neighborhoods where many people have pools or spas. Typically, they are clustered, and where you find one pool, you'll likely find others. Thus, hit these neighborhoods with direct mail coupons, or simply go door-to-door with flyers advertising your service.

How to Charge

Offer your services in a variety of ways, and make sure to be explicit about charges. You should have a flat fee, say, for a winterizing treatment. Your flyer should give a basic idea of the services that includes, and a price for the total treatment. You should also do installations of ozone generators or whatever other system you're looking to put in, and the manufacturer or wholesaler will give you a rough idea of how long it should take to install, and how much you can charge for it.

Your real gravy will likely come from continued maintenance contracts. Sign people up for a full year's service, including regular (weekly) vacuuming, checking of pH balance and other water quality indicators, filter trap cleanings, etc. In the case of a spa, offer to provide weekly or semiweekly water and filter cleanings, and regularly (for example, bimonthly) change the water. If you do use any retail products, charge your customers retail prices for them, though you should be able to get contractor and/or whole-sale discounts on them.

Other Helpful Hints and Advice

Legionnaires' disease and other biological health threats from pools and spas are real, though extremely rare. Be sure to have contracts with your clients that release you from any liability in these cases. Alternatively, take out a good insurance policy against this liability.

Manufacturing and Wholesale Production

- **Biodiesel Cooperative**
- **Gift Basket Service**
- **Organic Community-Supported Agriculture**

Biodiesel Cooperative
- Sell biodiesel fuel through retail and delivery

Description
A company can sell fuel for vehicles, heating, and other machinery at a fuel station or through delivery services. This type of company is effectively a middleman, buying fuel from wholesalers and delivering it to fleets, the general public, or a retail location.

Green It!
You can specialize in the distribution of biodiesel fuels. Biodiesel can be derived from canola (rapeseed), sunflower, or other oil-producing crops, recycled from used grease in restaurants, and hopefully in the near future, produced by algae and other low-impact methods. For more information on biodiesel fuels, see www.biodiesel.org.

A biodiesel cooperative taps into the growing interest in renewable fuels but also plays to the rising cost of traditional petroleum fuels. As biodiesel becomes more cost competitive, its use will only continue to grow.

Ecopreneurs in Action

Wesley Caddell and Ben Jordan of the Peoples' Fuel Cooperative in San Francisco, California, both point to the most important aspect of a successful cooperative: quality of fuels. If you can offer a consistently high quality fuel, they say, your customers will continue to come back to you. The Peoples' Fuel Cooperative has also earned consulting jobs setting up a quality control protocol for larger companies handling biodiesel.

Caddell also adds, "If you want to do this for the long haul, the model that works is small, local, sustainable." If you commit to sustainable biodiesel sources, as opposed to turning all arable land into biodiesel crops, "you'll always have a committed clientele," he says.

Getting Started

A group of committed individuals is crucial to beginning a co-op. These people, as well as their network of like-minded acquaintances, can all pitch in membership fees to provide start-up capital for the co-op. Typically, membership dues can be as low as $50 per year. In return, members get a small (for example, 10 percent) discount for shopping at the co-op. These first members will need to vote on whom to hire to manage the retail fuel location, or if a retail location is even necessary. Some co-ops offer members the chance to work four to eight hours per month on a committee in exchange for the discounted rate on a month's worth of biodiesel.

To begin, it is possible to buy biodiesel from homebrewers and sell it through the network of members. This is the lowest budget way to begin a cooperative, and it gives homebrewers a financial incentive to join the co-op. However, homebrewers cannot invest in the significant equipment necessary to ensure consistently top quality fuel, so in the long term, it is best to find wholesale manufacturers of biodiesel fuel and simply act as a middleman for them, finding customers to deliver to or providing a retail location (gas pump) for distributing fuel.

As things progress, you'll need an above-ground storage unit for your fuel, which may cost anywhere from $15,000 to $30,000, depending on size, location, and local regulations. This expense was cited as the main expenditure for a biodiesel fuel cooperative.

Finding Customers
- Flyers
  - Health food stores
  - Vegetarian restaurants
  - Coffee Shops
- Networking
  - Green Drinks
  - Drinking Liberally
  - EarthSave.org
- Press Releases

A variety of Web sites are tailored to the growing fan club of biodiesel maniacs, including www.biodiesel.org and www.biodieselamerica.org/biodiesel_coop_guide. Listing your co-op on these sites is advised.

How to Charge
The membership dues of most biodiesel co-ops are typically pretty minimal, in the range of $50 to $100 per year. Members should then receive a discount on fuels purchased, perhaps 20 to

30 cents per gallon. This discount provides members with an incentive to buy memberships and become active in the community. The margins on biodiesel sold through co-ops are not excessive, typically 20 to 40 cents per gallon. If you make deliveries, you should add a surcharge based on your delivery expenses.

Other Helpful Hints and Advice

As with most fuels, biodiesel is flammable, and it should be handled with care. Consult with your municipality on the storage requirements of large quantities of the fuel, and find out what regulatory hurdles you will need to deal with. Be ready to handle spills from the delivery truck and at your retail location. Your insurance agent should be able to set you up with any information you need about handling fuels, putting up signs, and filing materials safety data sheets (MSDSs).

Gift Basket Service

- Create decorative and attractive gift baskets.
- Select gift basket items that are organic, locally crafted, and eco-friendly.

Description

People who make gift baskets select a variety of nonperishable food items, put them together into some sort of package (not necessarily a basket), and sell them. They may sell these items anywhere from farmers' markets to retail locations, through florists (who may package them together with flowers) or through catalogs.

Green It!

Prepare gift boxes from recycled materials, or find a retail store that regularly disposes of the same kind of cardboard box and arrange to regularly pick them up. Decorate them with organic felts and fabrics if you can find them. Dress them up like wrapped gifts, and your customers will be able to reuse them again and again as gift boxes. This adds value to your package because people not only get a gift basket but they also get a wrapped gift box for their future gifting needs.

Pick items for your gift basket that are environmentally friendly. You can create a number of different gift baskets, giving them catchy names that are associated with what you will be putting inside them. For example, you may choose to do a chocoholic's organic orgasm, a gift box filled with all sorts of organic, shade grown, and Fair Trade chocolates and chocolate syrups for making mochas. Have a couple of great local organic food restaurants? Package a few of their nonperishable items and give your gift baskets "local" flavor. Organically grown dried fruits, triple certified coffees, and organically grown nuts are the best choices for food in your gift basket. You can also choose a variety of green consumer products, like pencils made of recycled money, organic cotton T-shirts, and the like. Your imagination is the limit!

Getting Started

You will want to source (research and find) the kinds of baskets and packages that are available to you, and how much each will cost to construct, make, or decorate. Keep it simple and choose one or, at most, two of these to use in your business to simplify your operations and help establish brand identity. Find out what kinds of foods and other gifts you want to include in your baskets. Try to include a number of items that you can purchase in bulk because that will save money. Put a sample gift basket together and compare it with other gift baskets sold in your area. This will give you an idea of how your baskets compare with those of your competition: whether your gift baskets are sufficiently full, overly full, diverse enough, attractive enough, and priced within the ballpark of the other baskets.

Finding Customers

- Flyers
  - Health food stores
  - Vegetarian restaurants
- Media outlets including those for niche markets
  - Local health and environmentally themed monthly magazines
- Booths
  - Farmers' markets

You should set up a Web site that gives details about your products and allows people to purchase them online. Find retail partners—for example, local shops such as florists that make deliveries and local organic food restaurants and health food stores that may agree to carry your gift baskets as long as they make a percentage on the sales. To establish these partnerships, you will have to meet with representatives from each place, show them your products, discuss inventory levels, and negotiate a fair cut for them.

How to Charge

Your retail distributors provide a terrific service to you in terms of distribution and promotion and in boosting the volume of your sales. In return, a healthy percentage of your profit should go to them. However, make sure you're still making enough margin to support your operations and to cover any unexpected costs, such as food spoilage and package damage.

Other Helpful Hints and Advice

Make sure you have checked with your state or local municipality regarding a food handler's permit. Also, put expiration dates on everything, even if the dates are a year in the future. If you have someone making deliveries for you (even if you are out-sourcing it to a local florist), make sure that the person is insured in the event of an accident. Remember also to consider food allergies, choking hazards, and the like. To get an idea of the legal and insurance issues involved, peruse some other gift baskets in your area to see what warnings and protections they have applied to their products.

....

Organic Community-Supported Agriculture

- Begin or take over an existing organic farm.
- Sell memberships to your community-supported agriculture (CSA) farm to customers interested in a regular supply of your fresh, local, organic produce.
- Sell the rest of your produce at local farmers' markets.

Description

Traditional farms have given way to the large tracts of agribusinesses. These large businesses have tried to apply business principles to the management of their land, resulting in a grotesque abuse of natural systems, chemical-dependent soils, semisterile ecosystems, monocultures, soil erosion, land degradation, and nutritionally depleted foods. Small family farms using conventional agricultural practices (chemical fertilizers, pesticides, and so on) have to compete with these agribusinesses on price, with predictable results.

Green It!

Small family farms are returning in the form of organic farms that offer Community Supported Agriculture (CSA). This business has grown tremendously; according to Local Harvest (www.localharvest.org/csa/), in the United States it has grown from an estimated 50 CSAs in 1990 to now over 1,500. Organic farmers can out-compete agribusinesses by producing a superior product: food that is real, chemical free, highly nutritious, tasty, and local. It takes several years to earn organic status, and the certification process is not an easy one. But if farming is a lifestyle you are interested in, it is not only a good alternative in terms of the health of you and your family but it is also a good business investment.

Selling your products directly to consumers at farmers' markets can help you make a better margin on them than if you sell them to grocery stores. Customers sign up to receive a bag of produce every week; customers either have the produce delivered to them, or they pick it up at the local farmers' market, which is recommended. Customers typically pay up front for the service, giving the farmer a pulse of cash in the off-season and reducing the risk of default. Then, if the CSA has a productive season, everybody wins. If something goes wrong and the farm doesn't have a productive year, customers may receive fewer fruits and veggies each week, but at least the farm doesn't go out of business. Usually, customers are very satisfied with the amount of produce they receive, and the farmer doesn't have to worry about a blight of locusts putting him or her out of business. This arrangement, in turn, guarantees that the farm will continue as organic, which many customers want to support anyway.

Ecopreneurs in Action

James Haggerty of Sun River Farms conducts business every Saturday morning throughout the summer at the Downtown Farmers' Market in Salt Lake City, Utah, selling his produce and divvying up his shares and half shares for customers of his CSA. Finding customers for his CSA is usually a matter of explaining the program to people who stop by his booth during the farmers' market just looking for some garlic, for which Sun River Farms is locally famous. The benefits of the CSA sell themselves, and many people sign up on the spot to get into the program.

Getting Started

You will need a decent amount of arable land, a way to irrigate it, some farm equipment, and workers to help with the harvest.

Experience with farming or gardening organically is also crucial. Knowing what organic fertilizers you can use, how to make and use compost, and where to get good-quality organic seeds will set you on your way to becoming an organic farmer. There is a great deal of information on the Web, and doing some research will help you learn. There is, of course, no substitute for getting out and getting your hands dirty, so consider doing a bit of volunteer work for a local organic farm before striking off on your own. Keep in touch with other organic farmers so that you can trade tips, strategies, and other information and perhaps share larger farm equipment so that you don't have to buy everything in your first year.

For more information about how to run a CSA, visit www.localharvest.org/csa.jsp. Jay North, an experienced organic farmer, has a Web site giving some useful information at www.goingorganic.com and travels worldwide to consult with people wishing to start an organic farm. Good reference books are *The Elements of Organic Gardening* by HRH The Prince of Wales and Stephanie Donaldson and *Rodale's Illustrated Encyclopedia of Organic Gardening* by Anna Kruger.

Finding Customers
- Flyers
  - Health food stores
  - Vegetarian restaurants
- Booths
  - Farmers' markets

How to Charge
Set up a couple of different size portions, called "shares," that people can "subscribe" to. A "half share" is typically one large shopping bag full of veggies and fruit. This amount is usually good for an individual or a couple. A "full share" is usually good for a family or an extended family, and it may include a couple of bags of produce.

Based on your farm's productive potential, you should sell as many shares as you think you can produce. Generating an extra $50,000 to $75,000 for a small or medium-sized farm based on revenues from the CSA should be adequate to keep you from going out of business if something bad happens and you don't have a productive year. Thus, you might consider selling half shares for $250 to $300 per year and full shares for $500. If your farm has a decent year, customers will save well over that amount for an equivalent amount of organic produce from the supermarket.

Other Helpful Hints and Advice

You should advise people to thoroughly wash veggies and fruits before eating them. While the risk of contamination is relatively low, it does exist (witness the spinach and green onion *Escherichia coli* epidemics in recent years). Contact an insurance agent to inquire about coverage. You'll also want to have worker's compensation and other related insurance if you are hiring workers to help with the harvest.

Personal Services

- Fitness Training and Diet Planning
- Green Real Estate Brokerage
- Green Shuttle Services
- Organic Food Delivery Services
- Organic Day Spa
- Travel Planning

Fitness Training and Diet Planning

- Support people in their effort to get and/or stay in shape through personal training, diet consulting, and personal menu preparation.
- Introduce people to sustainable personal issues such as toxin elimination and organic foods.

Description

People who offer fitness training will help coach a person to better health. They organize workout routines and schedules, guide clients through their exercises, encourage them to keep going, and find creative ways to reward them for hard work. Planning diets and personal menus helps clients take the training one step further, which is a more holistic approach to overall fitness.

Green It!

It is starting to be generally accepted that diets full of toxins can cause the body to retain fats (the body uses fat cells to isolate chemical or other toxins, so that their potential for harm is reduced). Thus, toxin elimination is becoming more and more of interest to people trying to lose fat and stay in shape. The carbon footprint of an obese person tends to be much higher than that of people of normal weight because they need bigger cars, they are unable to climb stairs and instead need escalators or elevators, and they consume more food and other products than necessary. Thus, helping people lose weight can help them in their personal sustainability as well.

Your goal in this endeavor would be to help people understand the link between conventionally grown foods, fast foods, and factory-farmed meats and the toxins they will deposit in your system. Many people have never been introduced to the topic of organic agriculture and avoiding toxin accumulation. Thus, you will plan their diets and menus according to healthier (and, coincidentally, more sustainable) agricultural practices that are centered on organic foods, free-range meats, and products free of artificial hormones.

Guiding clients to a more vegetarian lifestyle will also help eliminate toxins from their diet, as foods lower on the food chain tend to contain less environmental toxins than those at the top of the food chain, where toxins can bioaccumulate, especially in the fatty tissues of meats (for example, educate yourself about mercury toxicity in fish that are at the top of the aquatic food chain). Clients need not be entirely vegetarian, but you should definitely advocate more vegetables, whole grains, fruits, and nuts, and fewer meats, eggs, dairy products, and junk (processed) foods. This is not only healthier for the client but healthier for the planet as well, as the environmental benefits of a vegetarian diet are well documented.

Ecopreneurs in Action

Deanna McLaughlin of Health2Go! Fitness is the picture of health that she looks to promote. She has completed the grueling Wasatch 100 (a 100-mile run over seven major canyons in northern Utah) multiple times, and she promotes diet planning as just as important as fitness workouts. She has said that this holistic approach resonates well with clients who tend to be tired of miracle diets, fast fixes, and other short-term thinking in the fitness world. As a result, many clients have become advocates of healthy and organic foods, and they are keeping their physical fitness at its optimum level.

Getting Started

Experience in the diet and fitness arena will be quite helpful for this career. Your knowledge is important, but your experience with successful clients is perhaps equally or more important. You will also need to have a positive, can-do attitude and perhaps even some experience in coaching, so that you will be successful in a psychological way with your clients as well.

You can start the business in a variety of ways, including working with clients in their own homes (if they have workout equipment), their gyms, or in your own training facility. The latter is the most expensive way to start, though it allows you to cater to more potential clients, not just those who have gym memberships or home gyms. Also, the equipment itself will last a long time, thus this approach has lower long-term operating costs.

Finding Customers

- Web
  - www.WiseGrasshopper.com
- Media outlets including those for niche markets
  - Local health and environmentally themed monthly magazines

How to Charge

You can charge by the hour or offer multisession or monthly rates. Offer your clients a discount for multiple sessions. The longer the period they pay for, the more likely they are to stay with it, so try your best, for both your sakes, to get them on board for a month or more at least. If clients want diet training and meal preparation, you can add to the price for the extra service, and just tack the lesson on to the end of your workout session.

Rates for trainers and diet planners will vary widely depending on your locale, so look around at what other trainers are charging, and make sure you are not significantly different in your offerings.

Other Helpful Hints and Advice

Make sure you don't guarantee any results, but if you have "before and after" photos with other successful clients, let those photos and accompanying testimonials do the talking for you. An insurance agent should be able to help you understand all levels of your responsibility. If you are offering diet training and meal planning, make sure people understand the health risks associated with consuming uncooked meats, eggs, dairy products, and the like, and find out if clients have any special dietary restrictions such as gluten or lactose allergies.

Green Real Estate Brokerage

- Provide a similar service to other real estate companies, with a twist.
- Obtain certification as a green real estate broker if such certification is available in your area, and educate clients as to the green opportunities in each potential transaction.
- Donate a certain percentage of each commission to some strategic environmental objective.

Description

A real estate company helps buyers and sellers facilitate transactions related to land, houses, and other real estate. The company enters data for the properties into a searchable database so that other real estate brokers and agents can find them and show them to their own clients, they "stage" and show properties to potential buyers on appointment and through open houses, and they take care of the paperwork associated with transactions.

Green It!

Because there are so many real estate brokers and agents out there, this field of work can be particularly challenging to become successful in. Specializing as a green real estate agent or real estate company will help you corner a small niche market in a competitive marketplace. Many home buyers want to know the energy efficiency, chemical load, and other environmental data of their next home.

Some municipalities are offering green real estate broker certifications (sometimes called EcoBroker certification) that emphasize all the green attributes of real estate, including the extent to which properties adhere to common green building principles. See www.EcoBroker.com for more information. Emphasizing green priorities in real estate transactions will make you and your company a much more attractive choice to development companies designing, building, or managing environmentally sound developments. It will also make you a more attractive choice to anyone in the LOHAS community, which is a large and growing demographic of mostly upscale, professional, and educated potential clientele who also tend to be honest and serious consumers.

Another way to green up your real estate company is to specialize in properties that could use some greening and bring them to the attention of the environmental consumer. These may be vacant industrial sites, dilapidated downtown buildings, and other properties that are, in some way, degraded. Donating a portion of each sale to the environmental charity of your choice will also go a long way toward assuring your clients that you are the right real estate company for them.

Ecopreneurs in Action

Geoff McCabe of Tropisphere Realty hypothesizes that his company's green outlook has had a terrific impact on its bottom line. "We donate 10 percent of our gross commissions to local environmental, health, and educational organizations.... [This focus] sets us apart from our competitors in that potential clients [believe] that we must be more honest than other realtors who keep all their money.... Many sellers prefer to work with us to sell their properties." See www.tropisphere.com for more information.

Getting Started

Your personality and your personal network of connections are the most vital elements of success. Experience as a salesperson and attention to detail are traits often associated with successful real estate brokers and agents. Your knowledge of general and green building practices—for example, your knowing the differences between copper and lead plumbing—could also help you protect your clients from making bad investments (for more information, see www.usgbc.org).

A professional-looking office equipped with computers for clients to view some properties online is important to convey a sense of professionalism. A vehicle in which to take people around the area to view properties is also important, and if you want to cater to green clients, having a hybrid or alternative fuel vehicle is advisable. One very creative green real estate agent interviewed for this section also offers a bicycle tour around the city for willing clients.

Finding Customers

- Flyers
  - Health food stores
  - Vegetarian restaurants
  - Naturopathic physicians' offices
  - Area hotels
  - Metaphysical bookstores
- Networking
  - Green Drinks
  - Drinking Liberally
  - EarthSave.org
  - Sierra Club groups
  - Spiritual organizations
  - Outdoors clubs

How to Charge

Real estate brokerage fees are generally standard across the industry at 6 percent of the gross sale price. Typically, this fee is split between the realtor representing the buyer and the realtor representing the seller. Some organizations have different pay structures, so nothing is set in stone. However, as this is an industry standard, it might not be a bad idea to stick with what people are familiar and comfortable with.

Other Helpful Hints and Advice

It is very important to have contracts with all buyers and sellers detailing exactly what each party's responsibilities are. Real estate law firms specialize in this sort of thing, and they can help you protect yourself from potential liabilities.

Team Opportunities

Tropisphere Realty of Costa Rica is beginning a franchise program for people interested in living and working in Central America and trying to green the real estate market there. See www. tropisphere.com for more information.

....

Green Shuttle Services

- Shuttle tourists or locals between popular destinations.
- Use a diesel passenger van so that you can use B20 or B100 biodiesel fuel.

Description

Airport shuttles may be the most popular type of shuttle service, but a plethora of other types of opportunities exist. The idea is to find two or more destinations that are popular, and, for one reason or another, inconvenient or expensive for people using their own vehicles. What makes the airport shuttles so popular is that parking at an airport for a week while on vacation can be prohibitively expensive.

Shuttle services frequently cater to tourists or travelers, but there is no reason a shuttle service couldn't cater to commuters, mountain bikers, road cyclists, or any number of other customer types.

Green It!

By taking multiple passengers, you are basically creating a carpool. While this is a positive step in the green direction, you may also consider using a passenger van that has a diesel engine. That way, you can use biodiesel fuel. Check www.biodiesel.org for information and to see what types of fuel are available in your area.

Getting Started

You need a vehicle that can carry multiple passengers and a route for which people might be interested in using the service. Set a distinct schedule and keep to it, trying to cater to the kinds of people you will need as customers. Make sure you cover the major times of day or evening when people will need your service. There is no reason you could not continue to shuttle during the day, perhaps to and from the airport, train station, and bus station.

Finding Customers

- Web
  - ◦ Web logs (blogs)
- Media outlets including those for niche markets
  - ◦ Tourist maps and publications
- Networking
  - ◦ Outdoors clubs
- Press releases

The ways in which you find customers will depend largely on your choice of shuttle locations. If you decide to cater to tourists, you will have to have some sort of advertisement at the train station, bus station, and airport. If you want to do a bicycle shuttle run, advertising at bike shops is your best bet. You will get plenty of referrals because bikers tend to hang out with other bikers, commuters tend to know each other from the office, and so on. Don't forget hotel concierges, tour group operators, and meeting planners. You can network with these people and try to arrange extra jobs. Any time a convention is in your area, you can work the whole weekend, getting paid by the convention center or organizer and shuttling the conference attendees wherever they need you to go.

How to Charge

Most shuttle services charge per customer. You can arrange for monthly or weekly rates for regular customers. The major exception to the per customer fee schedule is if you are working for a conference or convention center. They will likely pay you for the service they can then offer to their attendees, who will likely offer tips as well.

Other Helpful Hints and Advice

You will have to apply for licenses with your local municipalities, and make sure you have adequate insurance on your vehicle to cover your business in the case of an accident. Make sure any drivers you hire have clean driving records and are careful first and foremost.

Organic Food Delivery Services

- Do the grocery shopping for busy professionals.
- Use a fuel-efficient or an alternative fuel vehicle to deliver the groceries to clients' homes.

Description

Busy professionals and higher-end clients hire grocery delivery services to do their weekly grocery shopping for them and then deliver the groceries and other items to their door.

Green It!

Most grocery delivery services operate on very thin margins. A terrific advantage of running this business as a green one is that you will be selling predominantly organic foods, which tends to mean a higher-end clientele, and thus a healthier margin (pun intended).

If you are lucky enough to have a locally owned health food retailer in town, see if he or she will give you a bulk discount (10 percent off your orders) because you will likely be spending a great deal of money in the store. The retailer may also do some preshopping for you, saving you a bunch of time and having a good amount of your nonperishable items already set aside, rung through the register, bagged, and ready to go when you come in. It's possible the retailer won't do any of these things for you, but it certainly doesn't hurt to ask.

Using a diesel Sprinter van (approximately 27 miles per gallon, biodiesel compatible, terrific storage capacity) or a small hybrid vehicle (up to 65 miles per gallon) will help you make this business as green as possible. You can also arrange to exchange cloth shopping bags with clients. They leave their empty ones for you, and you give them fresh ones with each food delivery.

Getting Started

Set up a schedule for each neighborhood to reduce your driving and to give clients a scheduled day to expect shipments. Food should be delivered before most people leave for work. This will help to alleviate concerns about spoilage and remove the guesswork of when groceries will show up.

You will need a vehicle. You would also benefit from having one or several large coolers in your vehicle to keep perishable items cold at the right temperature. You may need a place at your house or garage to store some bulk nonperishable items. Make sure it is pest-proof!

A good map of your community will help you find clients' houses. Alternatively, you may choose to get a GPS navigation system. Make sure you have plenty of cloth shopping bags to use and reuse for a variety of purposes. You can buy these in bulk, but your local thrift store is apt to have a dozen of these bags at any given time.

Your schedule will have to be fairly flexible because you'll have to work around the schedules of your busy clients. This may require working during the evening hours and during the weekends.

Finding Customers

- Flyers
  - Health food stores
  - Door-to-door in certain neighborhoods
  - Naturopathic physicians' offices
  - Bookstores

- Media outlets including those for niche markets
  - Local health and environmentally themed magazines
  - Co-op America
  - National Public Radio

How to Charge

You will want to make sure you have a good enough margin to cover your vehicle costs, your labor, and, of course, the cost of goods sold (the groceries you're buying). It's a fairly simple business, but the margins for traditional grocery delivery services have been low. Make sure you have reasonably accounted for all costs and that you can make a decent enough return to justify your efforts. The key is to have quite a few clients in one area. This type of efficiency will significantly help your bottom line.

Other Helpful Hints and Advice

Contact your insurance agent to discuss any coverage you may need for using a personal vehicle for the job. Have a lawyer draw up contracts for you. Be sure to include delivery expectations, release of responsibilities, and liability issues, and spell out that clients need to let you know immediately (same day) if there is a problem with food.

Team Opportunities

Door to Door Organics may be interested in helping you get started in your area (www.doortodoororganics.com).

Organic Day Spa

- Use organic products such as massage oils, facial cleansers, body products, manicure and pedicure agents, and bedding material (pillows, sheets, and so on) for the massage tables.
- Soften the mood with soy wax or beeswax candles with lead-free wicks.

Description

A day spa is a place of true rejuvenation, healing, and relaxation. Typically, a spa will offer a variety of services such as facials, waxing, massage, exfoliations, mud baths, manicures, and pedicures. Spas typically strive to have an atmosphere that is restful, calming, and peaceful, with separate rooms for massages, meditation, reflexology (foot massages), tea drinking, taking steam baths, soaking in hot tubs, and so on.

Spas typically create a menu of their services and offer packages to clients. Customers may wish to get a manicure and pedicure only, or they may instead opt for a full day of relaxation.

Green It!

A spa can be as green as you'd like it to be. There are many organic products on the market for a spa experience that is truly chemical free. Eminence Organics, for example, offers a pretty comprehensive line of organic spa treatment products, including enzyme peels, massage oils, facial creams, and body scrubs.

If you've ever felt lightheaded and weak after a soak in a hot tub, the problem may be more than just the heat: all that chlorine is volatizing and being breathed in by tub occupants. An organic day spa would ideally have a healthier hot tub experience. Greener options for cleansing a hot tub include ozonation, UV sterilization, industrial strength hydrogen peroxide, and mineral sanitizers. Tankless hot water heaters are the most energy efficient and inexpensive ways available for heating water.

The addition of organic massage oils, organic aromatherapy products, and organic cotton sheets for your massage table will add a special nontoxic and environmentally friendly touch to your practice. Use natural detergents to wash those sheets too so that you can keep them chlorine and bleach free. Candles made of soy, beeswax, or some alternative wax (as opposed to petroleum-based waxes), with natural wicks (as opposed to those with lead) will also add to your clients' sense of cleanliness and your commitment to their health and the environment.

Ecopreneurs in Action

Maryann Cockerille had a variety of debilitating health problems in 2000, but chose to make lemonade from lemons. "I learned about how to treat illness by changing your diet and doing different things, so I skipped some of the harsh treatments my doctor was recommending," says Cockerille. "I started doing yoga and eating a healthier diet. I wanted a chemical-free work environment, so I decided to create one in an organic, chemical-free way." Business is good, but most importantly, so is Cockerille's health. "I've never felt better," she says.

For more information about Cockerille's organic day spa in Fort Lauderdale, Florida, please visit www.BodyAndSoulRetreat.com.

Getting Started

While the potential financial rewards of a day spa are very good, the initial investment required is costly. Your sanctuary needs to be large enough to have several offerings, and that means several separate rooms. To get an idea of what kinds of things you'll need to have, visit a spa or two in your area. Privacy, serenity, and an elegant atmosphere help to create a great spa environment.

You might consider hiring an interior decorator and an architectural design firm to create your perfect spa layout. Some spas also incorporate outside space, such as Japanese gardens that you can see from some of the treatment rooms or patio sitting areas where people can decompress from the outside world before heading in for one of their treatments.

You'll have to hire massage therapists and purchase all the necessary equipment and supplies, such as massage tables, organic cotton sheets, towels, and robes. And if you've ever visited a spa, you know that the "nice touches" are a must-have—things like tea settings, placemats, flowers, and comfortable couches and pillows in the waiting area. Find companies that sell all of these products at www.coopamerica.org.

When you are ready with your building and your offerings, create a menu of services so that clients can pick out packages to suit their fancy. You might offer a page of skin care (peels, facials, and so on), a page of massages (deep tissue, four hand, couples, hot stone, pregnancy, and so on), a page of body therapies (scrubs, mud, seaweed wraps, masks, and so on), a page of hand and foot treatments (manicures and pedicures), and a page or two of "packages," which are basically combinations of several of the rest. Make sure you point out the green benefits of each of these services—after all, that is why customers will choose your spa over another.

Make sure you sell gift certificates! Day spa visits make terrific gifts, and they help to bring new traffic into your business.

Finding Customers

- Flyers
  - Health food stores
  - Naturopathic physicians' offices
  - Area hotels
  - Bookstores
- Media outlets including those for niche markets
  - Local health and environmentally themed monthly magazines
  - Co-op America
  - Tourist maps and publications

You'll need a Web site so that people can read about your chemical-free business, browse your luxurious offerings, and make reservations (and pay) online. Talk to local high-end hotels and green hotels (www.greenhotels.com) to see what kind of arrangements you can make with their front desk or concierge services. Keep a client list, and mail them coupons and special offers from time to time (on recycled paper, of course), especially for the holidays.

How to Charge

The cost of organic products has traditionally been higher than generic, chemical products. However, the gap is narrowing so you will not need to set your prices much higher than other spas in your area, if at all. Pick up a handful of other spas' menus, and set your prices accordingly.

Other Helpful Hints and Advice

Talk with an insurance agent for the details on what types of coverage your business will require. Have clients sign in and disclose any and all health concerns with their therapists, including injuries, allergies, sensitivities, and painful areas.

Travel Planning

- Organize vacations for clients based on their preferences.
- Set up wildlife watching, catch-and-release fishing, backpacking, National Park tours, or other environmentally friendly activities.
- Incorporate trains, boats, and bikes into your tour itineraries as often as possible rather than more polluting transport vehicles like airplanes or cars.
- Use green hotels and ecotourism companies to create total travel packages.

Description

Traditionally, travel agents are paid a commission by providers of travel services such as cruise operators. Thus, there is an inherent conflict of interest. A travel planner, however, makes money by planning a trip: what transportation option you might choose, what hotel you might stay in for how many days, what options you'll have during the day and evening for entertainment and so on.

Green It!

Your job would be to research the options and put them into a palatable and easily understood package, detailing lodging, transportation, meals, and entertainment, and then present the package to the client. After finding out what your clients' interests are, you can find green tourism resources just about anywhere.

Some reliable Web sites are www.SustainableTravelInternational. org, www.responsibletravel.com, www.SustainableTravel. com, and www.EcoTour.org. There are hotels certified as sustainable by the Green Hotel Association (www.greenhotels.com). Ecotourism operators exist just about everywhere there are tourists. Keep in mind the principles of green travel, such as Leave No Trace, and try to find operators that are truly committed to environmental protection and awareness.

Getting Started

This is a wonderful start-up business for someone who has enjoyed travel. While no actual experience is absolutely necessary, would you trust (pay) travel planners who had never traveled themselves? You should also read travel magazines and guidebooks to various countries and locales that focus on ecotourism (Northern California, Oregon, the National Parks, New Zealand, Iceland, Costa Rica, and so on).

There are few start-up costs other than a computer, a phone, and an Internet connection. You might also want subscriptions to travel magazines and environmental magazines (*E*, the *Environmental Magazine*, might be a good place to start). A new online magazine focusing on sustainable travel www.BelloMundo.com is also a good Web site to visit. Purchasing a variety of guidebooks to have a reference library at the ready is not a bad idea, though you can save this money by using your public library until you get enough clients to justify a larger library. In particular, the introduction, culture, and history sections of these guide books are full of information about each country's history of commitment to its people and its environment, and they will provide you with great talking points when meeting with clients.

Finding Customers

- Flyers
  - Vegetarian restaurants
  - Area hotels
  - Outdoor gear retailers
- Web
  - Facebook
  - Web logs (blogs)
- Media outlets including those for niche markets
  - Co-op America Foundation
  - Tourist maps and publications
- Networking
  - Outdoors clubs
- Press releases

How to Charge

You have two options: charge by the hour or by the job. You might want to start charging low fees, just until you get a reputation as a solid travel planner or until you decide to invest in an office so you look more official. As a good starting point, try not to charge more than 10 percent of the total cost of the trip.

Other Helpful Hints and Advice

Keep tabs on current health issues around the world, and don't send anyone where there is a potential health epidemic or political instability. The Peace Corps of the United States would be a great source of information about these topics because they have to vigilantly keep tabs on where their volunteers are and keep them safe.

Publishing and Related Businesses

- Environmental Freelance Writer
- Green Product Catalog Producer
- Publication Distribution Service

Environmental Freelance Writer

- Research and write articles, short stories, and books about environmental topics.

Description

Freelance writing is a terrific occupation for those with a wealth of experience in a particular topic and a knack for writing and doing research. Freelance writers are typically paid by the word for the work they create. Magazines and other periodicals pay freelance writers because it is usually far cheaper for them to pay an independent contractor than to keep writers on staff. They also frequently have topics they wish to cover that none of their writers have experience in.

Green It!

Focus your writing on an environmental field that you are an expert in.

Getting Started

You can set up this operation as a business in which you are an independent contractor for a variety of publications, which will then allow you to write off your business expenses. All you need to begin is a computer, an Internet connection, and a public library card. The more you plug yourself into the green community, the more you will be in touch with hot issues, like global warming, green business, green building, biofuels, and organic agriculture. Go to public gatherings, lectures, farmers' markets, green retail stores, natural food stores, and organic restaurants to absorb information. Check out books on environmental topics, and browse Web sites that are environmentally oriented (for example, www.enn.com or www.grist.org). Contributors to green blogs will be happy to talk about issues with you, which will help you gain varying perspectives and references to other research materials. Subscribe to *E*, the *Environmental Magazine*, one of the preeminent periodical sources of environmental education.

Once you feel comfortable with environmental issues, submit a proposal to publishers. Publishers typically prefer to have you submit a concept and proposal rather than a completed rough draft of your work. Viewing a proposal rather than a completed piece gives them time to work it into their publication and, if desired, to give you some subject matter to incorporate or consider. Don't be afraid to start small, with local, free publications. They tend to pay a lot less than publications with bigger audiences, but they are also less choosy in their publishing, which might help you get some valuable experience and build your résumé.

Finding Customers
- Direct sales

Head to the bookstore and peruse the magazine rack for magazines related to your area of interest (for example, biofuels). Make a spreadsheet listing the publications you are interested in, with fields for their name, contact, Web site, submission guidelines, and your comments. And then start submitting proposals!

How to Charge

Many publishers pay freelancers by the word. Others pay by the article. Most publishers have a fairly standard rate (which they usually post on their Web site) that they pay writers. So simply ask before you submit any work. As a general rule, publications with greater readership will pay more, but they are more selective when it comes to writers and subject matter.

Other Helpful Hints and Advice

As long as you make sure you've done your research and accurately identified your sources for information, you shouldn't have too much to worry about. Familiarize yourself with plagiarism, libel, and slander laws, and be careful not to overstep your bounds. You need to also consider the issue of "ownership" of your written material. This would become an issue if, for example, you eventually wanted to publish a book of your selected writings.

Green Product Catalog Producer

- Develop an attractive catalog of eco-friendly goods to distribute to lifestyle of health and sustainability (LOHAS) consumers.
- Partner with local green businesses to help them sell their products.

Description

General all-purpose catalogs of the old days are dinosaurs, and in today's marketplace they have been replaced by smaller, niche-market catalogs specializing in the products of interest to a particular group of consumers. Which is why creating a green product catalog could be the perfect small business for you.

In essence, running a catalog company requires creating a catalog, distributing it, and managing the sales from it. Some catalog companies sell their own inventory. That is, they are also involved in the purchase, storage, packaging, and shipping of the products in their catalog. However, a catalog company can also be run as a "middleman" business, meaning that sales orders come in from the catalog and the catalog company sends the orders to its wholesalers, who then package and ship the inventory. The catalog company makes a cut on the deal. Which type of catalog company you want to run is entirely up to you. Margins are higher on the first kind, but there is also a substantial amount of extra work. With the pace of business, it may be smarter to begin one in the latter category. You can also do a mix, in which case you handle some of the product orders yourself and pass off other orders to wholesalers.

Green It!

Putting together a catalog of entirely green products will put you into a profitable niche market. You can sell organic cotton clothing, recycled products, organic nonperishable foods, and the like. Partnering with local green businesses on this kind of endeavor can create a win-win situation for you both because they can sell more of their goods and you make a cut on each sale.

Print your catalog on 100 percent postconsumer recycled paper using soy-based inks, and purchase renewable energy credits from your public utility. These types of environmental commitments will prove to your customers that you are as ecofriendly as the products in your catalog; this will also go a long way toward endearing you to the LOHAS community. Alternatively, you can choose to put your catalog entirely online, saving yourself printing costs and saving paper as well.

Getting Started

Experience in the catalog industry would be very helpful, but it is not necessary. If you're not a designer, you can always hire one or bring one on as a business partner, but it is helpful to know your way around graphic design software. Publishing as a business has become vastly easier with the new software packages that are on the market. Adobe and Quark are commonly used publishing software for creating catalogs.

Other than that, you will need to know enough about the green marketplace to know what products people want and what's available. You will also need a good understanding of the green retail locations in town so that you will know what products people will buy from a catalog and what products people will choose to buy in a store. Knowing which products customers tend to purchase on the basis of the lowest price they can find would also be quite helpful. If some products don't sell, don't worry: you will constantly be changing, updating, and reevaluating your next catalog and its offerings.

Finding Customers
- Direct sales
- Networking
  - Green Drinks
  - EarthSave.org
  - Sierra Club groups
- Booths
  - Farmers' markets
- Press releases

You will have two types of customers. The first group will be the wholesalers of the products themselves. These folks will either pay you up front for the right to be in your catalog, or they will pay you based on how many sales you generate for them. If it is the former, you have a job of calling, meeting, and selling space in your catalog. If it is the latter, you merely have to contact them, get permission, and negotiate your cut.

The second group will be the users of the catalog. If you will be sending out these catalogs for free (this is recommended), you will need to target them to the greenest consumers around. You can send them via direct mail to the community with the highest number of LOHAS consumers (if you know your town, you likely know where most of these folks live). All you need for this type of mailing is to purchase a mailing list of this zip code or part of a zip code from a company that specializes in demographic analysis. Alternatively, you can get people to sign up for delivery and generate your own mailing list. Good places to reach the folks likely to sign up to receive your catalog are at booths at sustainability fairs, farmers' markets, and so on. You can also advertise and have them sign up via your Web site.

How to Charge

You can charge up front for wholesalers to put their items in your catalog. In this case, you will need to let them know how many catalogs you'll create and who will be getting them. This is very close to selling advertising, so make sure when you contact wholesalers they know the difference between your comprehensive offerings versus a traditional salesperson.

You can also charge a certain percent of each sale. It is a bit riskier, but if you're confident in your product (the catalog) and your wholesalers' products (items in the catalog), you can make it easy for consumers to purchase items through your Web site, after which you would send the purchase and shipping orders to the wholesalers themselves for processing.

You can also keep a supply of certain items and sell them directly.

Other Helpful Hints and Advice

You should pick up a variety of catalogs and look through them for shipping, packaging, and other information so that you can more or less match their offerings. If you are selling wholesalers' items, you will need to place the liability for shipping directly on them. Make sure you have protected yourself against the inevitability that a customer of the catalog will claim that some product never showed up from one of your wholesalers. Other considerations include the need for disclaimers on food items so that the responsibility for spoilage, leakage, and allergen warnings is placed directly on the company shipping the product.

....

Publication Distribution Service

- Distribute local publications to retail stores, coffee shops, restaurants, grocers, and other distribution points throughout the local area.
- By eliminating the need for each publisher to do its own distribution using its own car or truck, you are effectively creating a "publication carpool."
- Use a vehicle that operates on biodiesel, ethanol, or other biofuels or one that is very fuel efficient, like a hybrid.

Description

If you ever go into a coffee shop, take note of the pile of free publications available for customers. In any given city, there may be a weekly independent newspaper, a monthly health magazine, niche-market directories, underground music periodicals, theater publications, family-oriented monthlies, outdoor sports publications, and so on. Most of these publications are financed by advertising sales, thus making them free to the public. Most of them distribute to hundreds of local retail stores, coffee shops, grocers, restaurants, medical offices, and anywhere else people might pick them up. The better the distribution, the better the reach is for the publications' advertisers.

This distribution system is a great deal of work for the publishers, especially because they have to make sure to restock frequently so that they maintain a more or less continual presence. This system also costs a lot of money: in addition to paying for the driver and the vehicle, in many circumstances, publishers have to pay for the rights to distribute at particular locations. Publishers often cite this maintenance and upkeep as one of the biggest hassles of their job. Thus, many of these publishers would be quite happy to hire someone reliable to handle their distribution for them.

Your business would offer distribution services to a variety of these publishers. In exchange for their hiring you to specialize in handling their distribution and managing their locations database, they can focus on their areas of expertise, which are making a good publication and selling lots of advertising.

Green It!

You can create a "publication carpool" by getting hired by more than one of these publications. As many of them go to a lot of the same locations, it is far more efficient to have one vehicle handle the distribution for multiple publications. If you can sign up several publications, you will effectively be taking several cars off the road and replacing them with your vehicle. A good vehicle for this kind of service would be a Sprinter, which is a large van with good mileage and plenty of room to build shelves, and plenty of headroom so you can work in the back without crouching all day. Sprinters are available with a diesel engine so that you can use biodiesel fuel. The manufacturer is also testing plug-in hybrid Sprinter vans, which should be on the market in a few years.

Ecopreneurs in Action

Polycube Media uses biodiesel-powered delivery vehicles and covers 3,000 locations in Southern California. In addition to providing this service, Polycube feels it is important to keep a clean display rack, and sends clients digital pictures of their distribution activities. See www.polycubemedia.com for more information.

Getting Started

There is no experience necessary to begin this kind of business. All you need is a vehicle capable of moving around a lot of publications and a good knowledge of the area's roads and geography. Start-up costs may be somewhat high, depending on whether you need to buy a vehicle or not.

To make some extra money, you can also sell advertising on the outside of your vehicle. Your large delivery vehicle will be like a moving billboard—it will be hard not to look at it—and it may be a desirable advertising space for a lot of clients.

Another potential revenue stream exists and can be explored by creating organized racks in distribution points. You can offer to pay rent for this space to the owner of the retail store or other distribution location; the owner would likely be more than happy to (1) have someone organizing the establishment's usually unruly stack of free publications, and (2) get a small stipend for the space. In exchange, you get exclusive distribution rights for that location, so that the publications themselves have to rent that space from you. You then have the right to dispose of the other publications that try to use the space for free, so you can politely let them know that they have to pay you for the right to distribute at that location. It's very effective marketing; plus you are helping to keep distribution points clean and respectable.

Finding Customers

- Direct sales

You will need to call publishers directly to inquire whether they would like to hire you. This should not be a hard sell, though you are likely to find that publishers won't trust you with their entire distribution right away. When you start out, just let the publishers know your services are out there, and then call back once in a while to inquire whether they would like to hire you.

Note that when a publisher does decide to try out your service, it may ask you to do just a small part of its distribution for a short time. In that case, the publisher is probably feeling you out, making sure that you'll do an admirable job. If you do, perhaps the publisher will decide to hire you for the rest of its distribution. The keys to getting the client are (1) do the job well: if the publisher goes to the grocery store and sees its rack empty, you may lose that client; and (2) be as cheap or cheaper than the publisher's existing distribution cost.

Managing publication racks for retail stores and other types of locations will require you to talk to the owners of those establishments. You should have contracts made up and ready to hand to the owners of these distribution locations if you find that they are interested in this idea. Your contract needs to detail what your rights, responsibilities, and duties will be and how much you will pay the location owners in exchange for your exclusive rights to allow or disallow (and charge for) a publication's distribution in the owners' establishment.

How to Charge

Charge your publishing customers per drop. If they are weekly publications with 500 distribution locations, you can negotiate to get paid, just for example, 75 cents per drop point. That means that they are paying you only $375 per week. If they had to pay their own driver for 500 distribution points, plus reimbursement and maintenance on a vehicle, they would easily spend that much. Thus, your services are a bargain to them. If you happen to be handling distribution at those same 500 distribution points for another publication, you're now making $750 per week and not doing any extra driving.

Charge your advertising customers on a monthly basis, and set your rates somewhere in the ballpark with other similar advertising outlets. Give a pretty significant discount if someone signs on for several months (less maintenance for you, less work done on the advertisements on your vehicle, and so on). To get an idea of what "moving-billboard" ad space costs, call your local taxi company to find out how much the company charges for ad space on its cabs.

If you work out the organized distribution service, you can charge your publications for the right to distribute at various points based on the traffic that spot receives. If it's a high-volume store, like a grocery store or recreation outlet, you can likely charge more than you can for a naturopathic physician's office, which may see only 10 to 20 clients per day. Just make sure that you are charging enough to offset your rental fees to the distribution point itself, figuring that there may be only one or two publications signing on, at least initially.

Other Helpful Hints and Advice

An insurance agent will help you with vehicle coverage. If you hire a driver, get someone with a clean driving record.

Retail Food and Food Services

- Free-Range, Organic Fresh-Mex Restaurant
- Organic Coffee Shop
- Organic Juice and Smoothie Bar
- Organic Pizzeria
- Raw Food Bar
- Sustainable Buffet-Style Restaurant
- Vegan Café

Free-Range, Organic Fresh-Mex Restaurant

- Create a healthy fast-food revolution by providing organic rice, beans, and veggies, complemented by free-range, organic, and sustainable harvest meats.
- Package burritos, wraps, and tacos with the freshest ingredients to provide healthy and ecofriendly fast food for those on the go.

Description

The cuisine known as "fresh Mex" is taking America by storm. The fare usually consists of burritos, tacos, and wraps filled with beans, rice, cheese, guacamole, and veggies or meat (or both). Customers are then able to spice things up to their tastes at the salsa bar. Beverages (especially Mexican beer) rounds out the service. Fresh Mex is relatively healthy, very fast, and easy to wrap for to-go orders. For the business owner, these restaurants tend to be highly profitable. Beans and rice cost very little to make in huge quantities, and they make up the bulk of the ingredients in most dishes. Customers typically pay $6 to $8 for a burrito that might cost the business $2 to make.

Green It!

Offering certified organic beans and rice is a terrific environmental option, and it will add mere cents to the cost of making each burrito. Select organic or locally grown veggies that are typical to Mexican cuisine. Your tortillas can also be organic. Wraps can be made of organic romaine lettuce leaves for not much more than regular wraps, and they offer a nice alternative for calorie- or gluten-conscious customers.

The meats you offer will make the biggest environmental difference. Free-range meats, organic meats, and sustainably harvested seafood are all widely available, and though they cost a bit more than their alternatives, many customers are aware that they are not only more healthy (free of chemical residues and artificial hormones common in the meat industry) but are more eco-friendly as well. For information about sustainable fisheries, see the Marine Stewardship Council Web site (www.msc.org).

For to-go containers, you need only furnish a piece of recycled paper and/or recycled aluminum foil to wrap up your offerings. For those customers choosing to eat in the store, offer a place for used paper and food scraps (a bin that you will compost), and a recycling bin for used aluminum foil. Make sure you put up a sign that says the aluminum foil needs to be relatively clean in order to be effectively recycled.

Getting Started

You'll need to rent or buy a building suitable for a diner. You'll need all the basic commercial kitchen appliances like a big refrigerator, a spacious cooking area, large counters for prepping foods, storage bins, and plenty of pots, pans, cookware, and utensils. For the beans and rice, you will want to consider five-gallon or larger pots, as you will be making huge quantities of your two basic ingredients. Try a couple of different salsa recipes, and offer a variety to your customers at the salsa bar.

Finding Customers
- Location, location, location
- Flyers
  - Health food stores
  - Coffee shops
- Media outlets including those for niche markets
  - Local health and environmentally themed monthly magazines
  - Coupons and coupon books

You might also sponsor an event, like a triathlon, for which you would make an in-kind donation of food for the participants and volunteers, in exchange for a chance to put up your tent at the event and sell food to spectators, as well as putting your logo on the official race T-shirt. That kind of publicity goes far with the healthy and active crowd.

How to Charge
There will likely be other fresh-Mex restaurants in town, and you'll want to be in the ballpark with their prices. Even if you are offering free-range, organic meats, organic beans, rice, and veggies, and sustainable harvest seafood, you'll likely be able to still make money charging similar prices as other fresh-Mex establishments. Remember that volume sales are the key to profitability.

Other Helpful Hints and Advice
The usual food handlers' permits will be required. Label any dishes that have peanuts, wheat, or any other product that have allergy implications. As with any restaurant, cleanliness in the kitchen will go a long way toward keeping bacteria out of

your food. A sign in your restroom will likely be mandated for employees to wash their hands before returning to work. Salsas should be labeled for their spiciness because many customers do not want extremely hot salsas, and they would be unhappy if they tried something that ruined their meal because it was too hot.

Team Opportunities

Sharky's of Agoura Hills, California, is seeking franchisees to carry forth their mission of increasing the demand for sustainable fresh-Mex restaurants and food. See www.sharkys.com for more information.

Organic Coffee Shop

- Open a coffee shop serving certified coffee ("triple certified coffee" is organic, shade grown, and Fair Trade, for example), vegetarian-friendly soups and sandwiches, and organic baked goodies.
- Organize themed promotions like open-mic nights and fundraisers for local environmental nonprofit organizations.

Description

Coffee shops typically sell coffee, tea, baked goods, and simple fare like soups and sandwiches. They may be welcoming environments with comfy chairs, couches, fireplaces, and wireless Internet, or they may be more focused on drive-through or walk-through customers more interested in their caffeine fix than in hanging out.

Green It!

Coffee has become increasingly available in organic, shade grown, and/or Fair Trade certified wholesale varieties (for example, see www.caffeibis.com or www.bluebottlecoffee.net). "Organic" means the coffee was grown under certified organic agricultural standards (without chemical pesticides or fertilizers). Coffee certified as "shade grown" is cultivated under an existing canopy of trees, allowing the forest to remain essentially intact, providing wildlife habitat, carbon sequestration, and cooling shade in tropical regions. "Fair Trade" certification means that farmers and other laborers in emerging-economy countries are receiving a fair wage for their labor, better than they receive from large agribusiness companies. Triple certified coffee doesn't cost you that much more than other premium coffees, and otherwise it is not much different (taste, aroma, color, body, and so on). Loyal customers may also want to buy the coffee from you by the pound at a retail price because most likely their local grocers will not be carrying triple certified coffees.

You can either create your own organic baked goods or sell organic goods that you obtain from local bakeries in a cooperative deal. Soups, sandwiches, and other simple fare are easy enough to create even in modest kitchens, and they can add substantially to your bottom line. Make these vegetarian, or choose your meats from free-range and/or organic sources.

There are environmentally friendly takeout cups on the market, made primarily of recycled paper with a thin coating of wax. The use of these cups is a major improvement over the use of Styrofoam or plastic cups. You can also offer a discount if people bring their own mugs—before you fill these mugs with coffee, you can clean them out quickly and easily with a quick jet of hot water from your tea dispenser.

Ecopreneurs in Action

Meg Lynch of the Velo Rouge Café in San Francisco started her organic café because she saw a terrific connection between cyclists and coffee shops. "After leading cycling tours, and seeing how much cyclists enjoyed stopping for a cup of coffee during a long ride to refuel and socialize, I just saw this as a natural symbiotic relationship," she said. Velo Rouge is not only decorated with bikes and Tour de France posters, it also has a big bike rack out front. Lynch says her best marketing besides word-of-mouth has actually been sponsoring various events through the San Francisco Bike Coalition.

Getting Started

To start out, you can rent a small retail space—even a cursory kitchen would probably provide you with enough working space to make coffee, tea, espresso, lattes, sandwiches, and soups. Type the keywords "organic," "shade grown," "Fair Trade," "wholesale," and "coffee" into a search engine to find wholesalers. Find local partners wholesaling organic or vegetarian-friendly microwaveable burritos or baked goods that you can sell.

By working in a retail coffee shop for a month or two before opening your own, you will gain experience and learn the ropes before you're off on your own.

Finding Customers

- Location, location, location
- Flyers
  - Bird-related retail stores, such as Wild Birds Unlimited and Wild Bird Centers
- Media outlets including those for niche markets
  - Local health and environmentally themed monthly magazines

People tend to seek out places with free wireless Internet, which costs very little, so it is a good idea to put up a sign on your front door that indicates your available Wi-Fi. Customers who hang out and use Wi-Fi may spend more money in your shop due to the longer time they are in your establishment.

How to Charge

You will want to make a decent margin on your offerings. When you set up your prices, you can charge a small margin for your coffee with the expectation that the low coffee prices will entice many people to also buy soups, sandwiches, baked goods, and so on.

You can estimate how much running your store will cost you and how many cups of coffee you think you'll sell per day and then set your prices accordingly. Or you can set your prices similar to those of your competition, try to keep your other costs down, and hope for the best, adjusting your prices as you feel the need.

Other Helpful Hints and Advice

Things to keep in mind legally are the temperature of your beverages, allergy information, and sanitation in your kitchen. As a public place, you will also need insurance against people injuring themselves in your store and other types of liabilities. An insurance agent should be able to handle your needs.

Organic Juice and Smoothie Bar

- Open a small juice and smoothie shop serving healthy, organic fruit and vegetable concoctions.
- Use sustainable harvest products, like the Açai berry.

Description

Juices are made fresh from a variety of fruits and vegetables, processed through a small appliance known as a "juicer." Commercial juicers are bigger and far more powerful than juicers for the home. Smoothie bars typically use commercial blenders, which can whip up smoothies faster than you can pronounce *Açai* (it's ahh-sigh-EE). There are good smoothie recipes all over the Internet, though you'd likely have more fun just whipping up as many combinations as you can think of and keeping the good ones.

Basic ingredients would be ice, yogurt, and, of course, fruits and veggies of all kinds. Some smoothie bars also serve some basic food staples, like toasted bagel sandwiches—something that doesn't add significantly to the size of the kitchen or the cleanup needed.

The business model is one of the simplest in the food service industry. Blenders, icemakers, juicers, and perhaps toasters and dishwashers are about the only appliances needed. Juices and smoothies are served mostly for takeout or drive-through, which in comparison to eat-in restaurants, requires less square footage of rental space and less responsibility for cleaning and maintenance of the facility.

Green It!

Choose organic fruits and veggies for your juices and smoothies. This is a green and healthy option that people will likely be willing to pay more for. You can also choose local produce when possible, which is not shipped from thousands of miles away and therefore does not require a massive amount of fuel usage.

Some of the items you can add to smoothies actually help preserve rainforests: Açai berries are harvested wild from the rainforest of Brazil, often by the native peoples. This creates jobs for very impoverished people who might otherwise be tempted to decimate their forest for short-term gains. Triple certified coffees can add that bit of jolt to your smoothies, and they are grown under the shade of existing forests in Central and South America, providing jobs while preserving rainforest.

You can either create your own organic baked goods, or you can buy them from local bakeries. Sandwiches and other simple fare are easy enough to create even in modest kitchens, and they can add substantially to your bottom line. Make these vegetarian or choose your meats from free-range and/or organic sources.

As for the organic coffee shop described in the preceding section, you can serve customers using environmentally friendly takeout cups, made primarily of recycled paper with a thin coating of wax. These cups are a major improvement over Styrofoam or plastic cups.

Getting Started

A highly trafficked area is crucial. You won't be serving high-dollar items like lobster tails and bottles of wine, and therefore, you will have to make up the difference in volume. This means, in essence, that you will need to find a place where there will be many potential customers passing by regularly. A small space is usually sufficient, so worry less about interior design and more about traffic.

Finding Customers

- Location, location, location
- Flyers
  - Health food stores
  - Vegetarian restaurants
  - Naturopathic physicians' offices
  - Metaphysical bookstores
- Media outlets including those for niche markets
  - Local health and environment monthly magazines

How to Charge

Crunch some numbers to see how much it will cost you to make a smoothie or juice, including the cost of labor, cups, napkins, ingredients, and cleanup. Your margin on top of this will also have to cover your other overhead including refrigeration, advertising, and time spent purchasing fruits and veggies. You can tinker with your prices, but realize that when you do, you also have to change all your menus and flyers.

Many juice bars offer "add-ins" like ginseng, guarana, protein powders, bee pollen, or shots of wheatgrass juice that are stirred into the juices and smoothies. Typically they charge about a dollar for these add-ins.

Other Helpful Hints and Advice

Contact your local municipality for a food service permit. The permitting department will let you know your responsibilities for sanitation in your restaurant. Other issues with potential legal ramifications to keep in mind are the freshness of your beverages, allergy information, and sanitation in your kitchen. An insurance agent will help you cover your other liabilities.

....

Organic Pizzeria

- Serve healthy pizzas (you can offer gluten-free, raw, and vegan pizzas) with organic veggie and organic, hormone-free, free-range meat toppings.
- Provide delivery in your area with hybrid cars.
- Complement your offerings with organic beer and wine.

Description

Pizzerias typically serve pizza, hot and cold submarine sandwiches, salads, and beer, wine, and soda. Most deliver food within a limited geographic range either free (tip only) or for a nominal charge.

Green It!

Using organic and seasonal ingredients whenever possible will ensure that your pizzas are eco-friendly. While organic ingredients cost more, consumers have shown an increasing willingness to pay extra for menu items containing them. Additionally, bulk orders for many organic staples, like flour, sugar, tomatoes, olive oil, and many vegetables, are available in most areas, and they will help keep costs down. Many microbreweries offer organic beers, including New Belgium, Butte Creek, and Stone Mill, but try to find something local because shipping an organic beer across the country nullifies the environmental benefits of buying organic. Nothing complements organic pizza quite like an organic beer!

Print your menus on recycled paper, using soy-based ink. Another major step in creating an eco-friendly pizzeria is to offer delivery in a hybrid-electric car or other fuel-efficient vehicle.

Ecopreneurs in Action

Vaughn Lazar and partner Michael Gordon started Pizza Fusion as a way to fill a void they felt existed in the market for people looking to eat out or get delivery from an organic restaurant. They didn't stop at simply offering delicious, organic foods. Lazar and Gordon made sustainability a benchmark of Pizza Fusion.

The list of environmental commitments is impressive. Says Lazar, "Our buildings are LEED certified, our delivery cars are all company-owned hybrids, our ingredients are organic as much as possible, all of our uniforms are organic cotton, all cleaners used in the restaurant are earth friendly, natural pest control is used, we have heat exchange units on top of our stoves that heat our water, and the stores up north will also get their heat from there. Our paper products are 100 percent postconsumer recycled paper with soy inks, and alternative papers are used when possible (for example, our menus are on sugarcane pulp paper). Our takeout containers are biodegradable and compostable." But the best part? "Has to be the organic beer and wine," says Lazar, with a grin.

Getting Started

You'll need to rent or buy a building suitable for a restaurant. You'll need all the basic commercial kitchen appliances, like a big refrigerator, spacious cooking area, large counters for prepping foods, storage bins, and plenty of pots, pans, cookware, and utensils, plus a couple of pizza ovens. Learning to prepare and bake an organic pizza is similar to learning how to prepare and bake a conventional pizza. However, if you are offering gluten-free pizza, you may need to tweak the traditional dough recipe required for pizza. You might look up a gluten-free cookbook for ideas for your local climate and elevation.

Finding Customers
- Location, location, location
- Media outlets including those for niche markets
  - Local health and environmentally themed monthly magazines
  - Coupons and coupon books

If your community has a local green business directory, advertise in it. "Pizza" is one of the most commonly referenced listings in most directories. Community involvement is also a terrific opportunity: as any civic event, bike race, environmental fundraiser, or beach cleanup goes better with free pizza donated by the local organic pizzeria. If you are offering delivery services, your delivery car can be a "moving billboard" by putting a vehicle wrap on it with your name and phone number.

How to Charge
You'll have to figure out what your costs are per dish and set your prices accordingly. Remember to factor in enough of a cushion to cover your labor, your rent, your employees, your other overhead, and any spoilage and other accidents that may occur. A good general principle is to mark up the price of the finished food items by about 50 to 75 percent over the cost of ingredients. If you're offering organic food, let the customer know that it does cost a bit more for the ingredients, and if they want you to continue offering organics, they should anticipate slightly higher meal prices.

Other Helpful Hints and Advice

The usual food handlers' permits will be required. Contact the permitting departments of your municipality for further information about sanitation and other requirements. Label any dishes that have peanuts, wheat, or any other product that have allergy implications. If you are making deliveries, you'll want to make sure your vehicles are covered with the proper insurance for commercial use.

Team Opportunities

Pizza Fusion, an organic pizzeria headquartered in Fort Lauderdale, Florida, offers franchise opportunities to aspiring ecopreneurs. See www.pizzafusion.com for more details, or call (954) 202-1919.

Raw Food Bar

- Open a small takeout or deli-style restaurant serving raw (uncooked) foods.
- In addition to regular dining, sell packaged meals for busy people concerned about the health effects of cooked foods.

Description

Mainly for health reasons, interest in raw food has increased greatly. In essence, raw foods are the quintessential "whole foods" because they contain the nutrients, vitamins, and minerals they are meant to contain in the most natural state possible. Raw food preparation is quite different from traditional cooked food preparation. Not many people have much experience with raw food preparation, so there is a growing niche market for raw-sterateurs to open healthy diners based on serving raw food.

Green It!

Raw food is inherently green. It must be served very fresh, which means that more than likely it will be seasonal produce from local farmers that makes up the majority of your ingredients (this is also one of the secrets to the health benefits of raw food eating). It also requires little to no cooking in the traditional sense although some raw foods are warmed, and it produces very little waste. Raw foods are mostly vegan, which tends to be a very eco-friendly diet.

Your customers will be looking primarily for mostly organic ingredients, meaning your bulk food purchases will be supporting organic agriculture. Find compostable takeout containers, use cloth napkins, compost your scraps, and do all the other little things that can help make a restaurant green.

Ecopreneurs in Action

Omar Abou-Ismail of Living Cuisine, a raw food bar in Salt Lake City, Utah, says, "I love the people I meet who are very conscious and share their vibration, knowledge and wisdom." As for opening a raw food bar, he suggests that you have to be *talented* at making food, not just dedicated to making raw food. "Your food has to be incredible for [your clients] to come back. They have to want to lick the plates in order for them to come back again and again." Omar experimented with raw dishes at home to get experience before opening Living Cuisine, and suggests *The Complete Book of Raw Food: Healthy, Delicious Vegetarian Cuisine Made with Living Foods*, by Lori Baird and Julie Rodwell.

Getting Started

Educating yourself about raw food is the first step. Most of your customers will want to know about raw foods and why they should be incorporating more and more of them into their diet. A couple of main tenets should be sufficient. First, raw food is whole food. Second, there are few, if any, processing or artificial ingredients in most raw food dishes. And third, our species evolved with raw food diets for thousands of years, meaning that our internal biology is likely better equipped to digest, process, and absorb nutrients from it than from cooked food.

Develop a set menu of raw food items. You can find these in a variety of cookbooks on raw eating. A recommended edition is *Living in the Raw, Recipes for a Healthy Lifestyle,* by Rose Lee Calabro.

While you can learn what you need to know through books and experimentation in your own kitchen, it would be wise to find an existing raw food restaurant and ask if you can volunteer in that restaurant's kitchen for a while. You'll learn by doing, and gain the valuable insights of those who have been doing it commercially for a while, so that you can avoid the pitfalls they encountered.

If you can find a raw food restaurant in your own town, make sure you are honest and up front with the owner of that restaurant that you are thinking of opening your own place. Odds are, the person you are volunteering for will be excited to find another pea in his or her pod. Perhaps you two can partner up in creating another restaurant, or at the very least you can send customers back and forth. It is possible, however, that the person will resent the competition you present, especially if you plan to open your place in the same part of town. If there is no raw food restaurant in your area and you still want to work in someone else's kitchen before diving into your own, do some online research and find others around the country, then decide if you'd like to go and live somewhere else for a little while so you can learn the art of raw food.

Your restaurant does not need to be large. You can make a good deal of money on takeout items so you won't need as many seating areas.

Start-up costs are not excessive. You'll need a couple of commercial refrigerators, a variety of sprouting jars and trays, blenders, glass jars with lids (for soaking nuts, beans, and sprouts), and the usual kitchen implements of mixing bowls, cutting boards, utensils, and the like. Since there is no stove or oven, your kitchen will remain a nice ambient temperature year round, making it a nice place to work as well, and saving you space in your kitchen and money on your utilities.

Finding Customers
- Location, location, location
- Flyers
  - Health food stores
  - Naturopathic physicians' offices
  - Metaphysical bookstores
- Media outlets including those for niche markets
  - Local health and environmentally themed monthly magazines

Many health food stores offer community education classes, so see if you can teach one about raw food preparation. Each month, do a class about a new dish, showing people how to prepare it. In the meantime, you get to spread awareness of raw food, and, more importantly, your restaurant!

How to Charge
You'll have to figure out what your costs are per dish and set your prices accordingly. Remember to factor in enough of a cushion to cover your labor, your rent, your employees, your other overhead, and any spoilage and other accidents that may occur. A good general principle is to mark up the price of the items by about 100 to 150 percent over the cost of ingredients. You'll likely offer full meals for $15 to $20.

Other Helpful Hints and Advice
Check with your municipality to see what your sanitation requirements are. Label any dishes that have peanuts, wheat, or any other product that has allergy implications. If you are growing sprouts, make sure you do it properly, washing them twice per day during

their growth, as molds and other contaminants can occur readily otherwise.

. . . .

Sustainable Buffet-Style Restaurant

- Open a menu-less café serving a variety of soups, cold salads, hot dishes, and desserts based on seasonal and organic ingredients.
- Allow customers to choose their own portions and price their own meals, with the goal to eliminate food waste.
- Use donated items, such as bowls, mugs, serving trays, silverware, pots, pans, furniture, decorations, and even larger items like appliances and a piano.

Description

Buffet-style restaurants allow customers to take whatever food they want in whatever portions they want, and they typically make a set price for the entire meal, no matter how much someone eats.

Green It!

To discourage overconsumption and food waste, allow customers to choose not only their own portion sizes but also their own prices. Trust them that if they take more food, they will tend to pay more for the meal.

Having no menu allows you to make whatever food is local, seasonal, and readily available. This means the food will tend to be less expensive, fresher, more nutritious, and environmentally friendly. It also means your chef will be able to use creative energy on a daily basis rather than making the same dishes over and over. Customers know that organic costs more, and they will hopefully appreciate your commitment by adding a few bucks to the price they pay.

Your dessert, the "Everything Cookie," will be part of a recycling effort, where yesterday's fruit, nuts, used oil, and other ingredients become part of one giant cookie that you cut into portions as dessert for today's customers. This cookie, in fact, is the only thing that is on the "menu" every day!

To complete the eclectic, green, and community feel of the restaurant, ask customers to donate items they no longer need, such as plates, bowls, spoons, pots, and pans. You can arrange with farmers for you to pick up excess produce left over after the morning farmers' market, which saves them hauling it back home and composting it. Put up a wish list for items, and update it frequently based on your desires for the restaurant.

Ecopreneurs in Action

Denise Cerreta is the founder of the One World Everybody Eats (OWEE) Foundation, through which she also founded the One World Café in downtown Salt Lake City, Utah. The café was the very first sustainable buffet-style restaurant of this type.

Cerreta has said that starting her paradigm-shattering restaurant felt sort of like jumping off the rim of the Grand Canyon: "I was sure I would splat at the bottom." However, four years later, the One World Café in Salt Lake City continues to thrive, and it has become a community institution—not only in Salt Lake but around the world because the model is spreading through the OWEE Foundation. "OWEE truly wants to help humanity. We believe that anybody who wants to do this type of work will be making a real difference and a significant contribution to the world in their lifetime," says Cerreta, "and now that I and others have done it, I suggest you take the leap. We are at the bottom looking up at you. Our experience can be your safety net. We've done it, and it can work."

Getting Started

You can rent a small retail space and furnish it with donations from your own collection or from friends' houses (these can be borrowed until suitable replacements are donated by customers). Thrift stores also have a variety of decent secondhand goods you can use to equip the kitchen and dining areas. The One World Café model uses two 5-gallon soup warmers, a half dozen or so cold salads on serving trays in a thin tray of ice, and a four-compartment warm server for hot dishes. These are served by staff from behind the buffet line. Coffee, tea, and cold drinks are self-serve outside the buffet line and kitchen area. Customers bus their own tables and bring the plates, bowls, and silverware back to the kitchen. All of this adds up to a very low budget start-up.

Recipes are available on the One World Café Web site, and the business idea is free for the taking, as long as the entrepreneur carries forth in the mindset of sustainability, elimination of food waste, and ending hunger. At time of publication, the model had been successfully run in Salt Lake City and Denver, and plans were in the works for New York City, Washington, D.C., Minneapolis-St. Paul, Iowa City, Boston, Santa Fe, Philadelphia, Atlanta, Fort Lauderdale, and Chicago.

The donation model has been so successful in Salt Lake that someone even donated a plot of valuable land in downtown Salt Lake City to be converted to an organic garden to produce part of the restaurant's veggies and to compost food scraps!

Finding Customers

- Location, location, location
- Flyers
  - Health food stores
  - Metaphysical bookstores
  - Coffee shops
  - Outdoor gear retailers

- Media outlets including those for niche markets
  - Local health and environment monthly magazines
- Press releases

How to Charge

Suggest prices for a variety of meal types (for example, "coffee and dessert only: $5, full meal of soup, salad, main course, dessert and beverage: $10 to $15"). You can also offer catering services using the same kind of price structure, suggesting a price and trusting your clients to follow through.

Other Helpful Hints and Advice

Your municipality will let you know your obligations in terms of sanitation, signage, and food-borne illness prevention. The usual liability insurance and worker's compensation are the basic insurance requirements.

Team Opportunities

The entire business model can be downloaded as a PDF file from www.oneworldeverybodyeats.com. The One World Everybody Eats Foundation can be contacted through this Web site, and this may be an invaluable resource for someone wishing to start a sustainable buffet-style restaurant like this. The foundation may help you pick a location, get a crew together, and walk you through the process, and it may be able to help provide financial support.

....

Vegan Café

- Start a mini revolution by creating scrumptious vegan delights.
- Network through the highly loyal vegan community to establish a regular customer base.

Description

A specialty food café such as this one offers customers a product that appeals to their specific tastes. This is one of the major benefits of a specialty café: it engenders a fairly loyal base of customers in that particular community. It also helps the business owner concentrate his or her marketing efforts and dollars in the most effective way.

Green It!

A diet consisting of foods lower on the food chain is a more eco-friendly diet. For example, the global warming caused by methane from cows in the United States is equivalent to about 33 million cars. Sixty to seventy percent of rainforest destruction in Brazil is done to clear land for cattle. The United Nations reports that livestock production causes 55 percent of all soil erosion worldwide, is responsible for 37 percent of all pesticide usage, and 50 percent of all antibiotic usage. In addition to being more eco-friendly, a vegetarian/vegan diet provides specific health benefits, such as reducing the risk of heart disease, certain cancers, high cholesterol, high blood pressure, and diabetes. For further information on the environmental and health benefits of a vegan diet, check out *The Eco-Foods Guide*, by Cynthia Barstow; www.vegan.org; and www.tryvegetarian.org.

You can grow a lot of sprouts for use in a variety of your dishes, which is an extremely environmentally friendly way to produce food. Think of it as your own little organic indoor garden that you can "farm" all year round. It costs a lot less than buying sprouts, and it provides a little more freshness and flavor in your cuisine.

You can also use mostly organic ingredients, find compostable takeout containers, use cloth napkins, compost your scraps, and do all the other little things that can help make a restaurant green.

Ecopreneurs in Action

Ian Brandt, proprietor of Sage's Café, a 100 percent vegan and mostly organic food restaurant in Salt Lake City, recently decided to expand Sage's by opening a second vegan café in Salt Lake. If a vegan restaurant can not only succeed but also expand in a state as conservative as Utah, there is no reason it can't succeed anywhere as long as the food is good and reasonably priced.

See a sampling of Brandt's scrumptious cuisine in his upcoming book *Revolution Cuisine* (Gibbs Smith Publishers, www.RevolutionCuisine.com). The peanut butter fudge brownie with soy French vanilla ice cream and dark chocolate glaze is perhaps the finest dessert this vegetarian author has ever had!

Getting Started

You'll need to rent or buy a building suitable for a diner. You'll need the basic commercial kitchen appliances, a spacious cooking area, large counters for prepping foods, storage bins, and plenty of pots, pans, cookware, and utensils.

To learn about vegan food preparation, you can browse your local bookstore for a vegan cookbook or search the Web (try www.vegcooking.com) to look for inspiration and recipes.

Endeavor to hire mostly vegan or vegetarian employees because they will be the most experienced and knowledgeable ambassadors about the foods you are serving.

Finding Customers

- Location, location, location
- Flyers
  - Health food stores
  - Bookstores
  - Coffee shops
- Media outlets including those for niche markets
  - Local health and environmentally themed monthly magazines

- Networking
  - EarthSave.org

Circulate flyers within and sponsor fundraisers for vegan organizations, animal lovers groups, and environmental organizations.

How to Charge

You'll have to figure out what your costs are per dish and set your
prices accordingly. Remember to factor in enough of a cushion to
cover your labor, rent, employees, other overhead, and any
spoilage and other accidents that may occur. A good general principle is to mark up the price of the finished food items by about
50 to 75 percent over the cost of ingredients. This should allow
you to charge a decent price for a more than decent meal.

Other Helpful Hints and Advice

Your municipality will have information on all the rules and
regulations for running a restaurant in your area, including
sanitation standards.

Retail Nonfood Operations

- Alternative Transportation Retail Store
- Aveda Concept Salon
- Bike Shop
- Consignment Store
- Edible and Organic "Floral" Arrangements
- Green Building Supply Store
- Green Product Retail Store
- Native and Organic Plant Nursery
- Printer Cartridge Refilling Store
- Used-Book Exchange

Alternative Transportation Retail Store

- Open a retail shop selling commuter bikes, electric bikes, electric scooters, high-efficiency gas scooters, and other ecofriendly transportation alternatives.
- Maintain an online retail presence selling kits for electric bikes.

Description

Everyone needs transportation. Bikes, skateboards, cars, motorcycles, and scooters all fit the bill, and depending on road conditions, weather, and personal preference, each has a specific utility.

Green It!

A retail store specializing in eco-friendly transportation solutions can have a tremendous impact on the environment. And the best part is that there is a variety of alternatives. Commuter bikes are more rugged than road bikes, with a bit more tread and the ability to take a beating from potholes, curbs, and other uneven surfaces. They can be fit with saddlebags (a.k.a. *panniers*) that allow a rider to carry evenly distributed weight without having to wear a backpack.

Bikes can be made electric as well. Special kits affix a motor, typically to the hub of the tire, and include a rechargeable battery pack. Efficiencies vary, but most models on the market can go 20 miles per hour, and they have a range of about 20 miles per charge. Your retail store could sell bikes already fit with electric motors and install the kits if customers want to add motors to an existing bike. You can also sell the motor kits to do-it-yourselfers, both through the retail store and online.

Electric scooters are becoming more viable as transportation alternatives. Like electric bikes, they save consumers quite a bit of money because they don't use gas, and they have zero emissions when they are being ridden. Even if you are charging these electric scooters and bikes on coal-generated electricity, they are far more efficient per mile than their gas-powered counterparts.

Gas scooters are efficient transportation alternatives as well, frequently getting up to 100 miles per gallon. Engines of 150 cubic centimeters (cc) tend to get about 75 miles per gallon, and they can be ridden at speeds of up to 55 or 60 miles per hour.

At time of publication, electric all-terrain vehicles (ATVs) were entering the market, and they would make a good addition to your retail selection if you live in an area with a lot of dirt roads, uneven terrain, or mountain recreation opportunities. There are also small electric cars, and you might want to stock a few of these as well.

Ecopreneurs in Action

Eco-Moto, a Salt Lake City–based alternative transportation retail store, credits online sales for a good proportion of its revenues. Jon Schlee, owner of Eco-Moto, says that electric hub motor installation kits for the do-it-yourselfers interested in electrifying their bicycle commutes are hot Internet sellers. Schlee originally opened his store in the University District to capitalize on student business, and he finds that expos and shows, where people can see, touch, and ride his products, are the best advertising. See www.eco-moto.com for more information.

Getting Started

It goes without saying that it would be helpful to be familiar with the various options available for eco-friendly modes of transportation. You will want to test each type of method (of course you will ... this is part of the fun of running this kind of business!). Make sure either you or someone you hire can fix your products.

You will need a decent amount of capital to begin this business. The inventory itself is fairly expensive (imagine a small showroom full of scooters and electric bikes), on top other expenses like rent, advertising, employees, and the costs involved in setting up a small workshop in the back of the store.

A business like this will do especially well in college and university towns, larger cities, downtown environments, and in beach areas. This does not mean, however, that it cannot succeed in the suburbs. Parents may be looking for an alternative for their children to commute to school, and since electric bikes don't require licenses in most states, these make great commuter vehicles.

Finding Customers

- Location, location, location
- Flyers
  - Coffee shops

- Media outlets including those for niche markets
  - Local health and environmentally themed monthly magazines
  - Co-op America Foundation
- Booths
  - Farmers' markets
- Press releases

You can create buzz by stocking some inventory outside the store, which will allow passers-by to "kick the tires" and become curious. Your products will be pretty different, and of course, fun, so people will likely tell their friends about them. As people begin riding them around town, they will get plenty of looks and questions about where they bought them.

Another terrific opportunity is to have a local radio station do a live show from your parking lot. It is good exposure for them and, obviously, for you as well, and it can frequently be arranged fairly easily. Radio stations do this kind of promotion for auto dealerships all the time, giving away bumper stickers, T-shirts, prizes, and refreshments to people who show up.

How to Charge

Manufacturers of these products will suggest retail prices (MSRPs—manufacturer's suggested retail prices). From there, you can offer sales and discounts as you desire. If you want, you can keep your margins slightly lower on your more eco-friendly products (commuter bikes) and a little higher on your less eco-friendly products (gas scooters).

You can make more money if you sell accessories with your products. Once someone has decided to buy a transportation alternative from you, you should endeavor to complete the purchase experience by offering options and accessories. This will not only improve your bottom line but it will also enhance the buyer's experience with the new product and increase the buyer's enjoyment of it.

There is, of course, a fine balance between making someone's purchase more complete and being a pushy add-on salesperson, the latter of which quickly garnering you a reputation you don't want. So offer the options but let people make up their own minds without being pushy about it, and you'll do fine. Remember that these folks will become your best advertisements if they are happy customers.

Other Helpful Hints and Advice

If you are allowing people to test ride your products, you will want to make them sign a waiver of liability and wear protective gear, and you will also want to hold onto their credit card or some other deposit while they're riding your products. There are insurance issues with test rides as well, and checking with an agent for local rules and regulations is your best bet. You may also want to find out if you should require liability waivers with each sale as well.

....

Aveda Concept Salon

- Open a salon based on the eco-friendly products of Aveda.
- Offer a range of services, including haircuts, perms, colors, manicures, and pedicures.
- Green your salon further by incorporating fundamentals of green building, making your indoor air environment as healthy as it is environmentally friendly.

Description

Traditionally, salons have offered hair treatments—colors, cuts, styles, and so on—and they still do. But today many are also branching out into massage, pedicures, manicures, and other personal services.

Green It!

Start an Aveda Concept Salon by partnering with Aveda, a world-class green business. Aveda sells organic, healthy, and earth-friendly hair and skin care products, perfumes (the company calls them

"Pure-fumes"), makeup, and gifts. Aveda uses plant-based alternatives to chemical ingredients, and it is committed to eco-friendly packaging. The company endeavors to source its products through socially sound agreements, and it purchases renewable energy credits to offset 100 percent of its energy use. In addition, Aveda has donated millions through various eco-awareness outreach campaigns. The company's commitment to purity and the high quality of its products are recognized internationally.

Partnering with Aveda gives you a terrific lineup of high-end products that sell well. It also gives you access to great clientele, many of whom will find out about your salon through the Aveda Web site or through Aveda's well-branded advertising campaigns.

Set up your building to be as free of volatile organic compounds (VOCs) as possible. This will contribute to your customers' experience of purity that they've come to expect from Aveda. It will also make a healthier work space for you and your employees. You can do this by using nontoxic paints, sealants, plasters, and other green building materials, as well as by opening the windows and letting the place breathe when the weather is nice outside.

Ecopreneurs in Action

"What brought me to Aveda was [Aveda founder] Horst [Rechelbacher]'s vision for saving the Earth," says Van Council of Van Michael Salon in Atlanta, Georgia. "Being associated with Aveda from the beginning helped us to take off quickly.... The power of the branding is huge. New people walk in looking for the product, and that helps the bottom line."

Getting Started

Aveda has a network of Aveda Institutes (these can be found on the Aveda Web site) where you can learn everything there is to know about running one of their concept salons. Once qualified, you can open a very modest salon or a much bigger space, depending on your level of comfort and financial commitment. Take a walk around some other Aveda Concept Salons (find them online at www.aveda.com, then click on "Find a Location") to get an idea of the peace and tranquility of the environment, as well as the offerings, prices, and organization of the business.

Finding Customers

- Media outlets including those for niche markets
  - Local health and environmentally themed monthly magazines
  - National Public Radio

You may also want to selectively advertise in local publications and other media outlets whose demographic is mostly women.

How to Charge

The products themselves will come labeled with suggested retail prices. What you charge for services is largely up to you, and your prices will be based on your cost structure and the cost of living in your area. A good idea is to research other salons in your area, to see what they are charging and what amenities they have, and to set your rates somewhere in that ballpark, or perhaps a little higher because you're offering superior products and (hopefully) services.

Other Helpful Hints and Advice

You'll need to have the insurance coverage that is customary for anyone running a retail operation. Contact an agent for more information.

Bike Shop

- Sell bikes and bike accessories in a retail store.

- Specialize in commuter bikes, allocating a significant part of your retail area to commuter bikes and commuter bike accessories.
- Provide support for bike commuters, including maps of bike lanes, bike-pooling clubs, and basic mechanics classes specifically tailored to commuters and their bikes.

Description

Bike shops sell bikes and bike accessories, including clothing, footwear, helmets, tools, lubes, degreasers, lights and other safety gear, bike computers, and all sorts of other gadgets for making your ride more safe and fun.

Bike shops can either get boxes full of parts and put the bikes together themselves (it's cheaper to ship that way), or they can have another company put the bikes together. Most bike shops also offer repair services, in which they get the chance to charge for mechanic service and also for parts off their retail shelves.

In order to compete with larger retail stores that sell bikes, small, independent bike shops may choose to specialize in a certain type of bike or a certain type of rider. This may include trick and/or stunt bikes, mountain bikes, road racing bikes, and commuter bikes. This doesn't mean that those are the only types of bikes and accessories these stores offer, just that they are known for these specialty bikes.

Green It!

While biking is, by its very nature, an eco-friendly activity, a bike shop that specializes in commuter and road bikes can help make it easier for workers to get to and from work without gasoline. Bike commuting is becoming more and more popular, thanks in no small part to the rising cost of owning and operating a vehicle. The benefits of bicycle commuting are awe inspiring: it is the most efficient conversion of energy to distance covered of any kind of travel (including walking!), it produces little to no waste products, it makes no significant noise, it needs a fraction of the maintenance and upkeep of cars, and it is good for the rider's health.

Ecopreneurs in Action

Mark Sunday of Saturday Cycles started his bike shop to awaken interest in bicycle commuting as an ecofriendly transportation alternative. Saturday Cycles specializes in bikes for commuters and touring, and it offers Rivendell, Heron, Soma, Surly, and Bianchi bikes, plus all the accessories needed for bike commuting, like *panniers* (saddlebags), lights, helmets, gloves, etc. See www.saturdaycycles.com.

Getting Started

Give some real thought to whether your town's roads are commuter bike friendly before you proceed with this business. You are likely to succeed if there are bike lanes, organizations promoting bike awareness, one or more college campuses, and an environmentally conscientious citizenry.

You will need a retail location, preferably one that is along the main commuter route to and from downtown. This will give you an advantage in terms of your main customers' not having to go out of their way to pick up some parts or get a quick tune-up.

Experience working in a bike store would be helpful. Perhaps take three months and work full-time at a local store, learning everything you can. You can also just jump in, however, if you can hire a manager with some bike retail experience. The same goes for an experienced mechanic, who can really make or break a bike shop.

A bike shop specializing in commuter bikes may carry bikes made by Breezer, Incline, Dynamic, Broadway, Biria, Specialized, Bianchi, Trek, and a variety of other bike manufacturers. Trek, Giant, Specialized, Kona, and Cannondale are larger bike manufacturers that have responded to market demand and started introducing commuter bikes, so expect to see the market for this kind of bike continue to grow. Information on each commuter bike is available from the manufacturer's Web site.

Your store should carry every gadget and accessory to make cycle commuting as comfortable as possible. Rear and front racks can be affixed to bikes so that people can ride with *panniers* on the side of their bikes' wheels. *Panniers* can carry a lot of gear and equipment, including briefcases, laptops, extra clothes, spare tires, portable bike pumps, and patch kits, Bikes should be equipped with front and rear lights for visibility in traffic, and riders should be encouraged to buy reflective clothing (vests, especially) that will improve odds of their being seen by drivers.

Make sure your store has up-to-date maps on all the bike lanes around town as well as maps of any trails people can ride as part of their daily commute.

Set up a workshop so that you can assemble bikes that come in from wholesalers and for making repairs to bikes brought to you by customers. A workshop will help add to your bottom line significantly, and it will also help you sell bikes because it will enable you to then offer one free tune-up within the year of purchase. You might consider buying and selling used bikes, in which case, you can buy a bike, fix it up, and sell it for a tidy profit.

Another thing to consider is that, depending on your local climate, many bike commuters may stop bike commuting in the winter. Thus, you will need to evaluate whether you should stay open during the winter. If so, you should perhaps offer other services such as selling and tuning cross-country skis and selling cycle trainers.

Finding Customers
- Flyers
  - Health food stores
  - Vegetarian restaurants
  - Coffee shops
- Media outlets including those for niche markets
  - Local health and environmentally themed monthly magazines

If your city has a bike commuter discount program, offer discounts to the group as a way of getting your name out there. Attend meetings of bike advocacy groups (it'll be great public relations). Offer to organize group commuting either by getting a signup list together or by having a bulletin board specifically catering to those wishing to find another commuter to ride with. This will engender some customer loyalty as well, and it will encourage commuters to come into your store frequently to check the board.

How to Charge
Manufacturers of bicycles will have suggested retail prices for their bikes, thus taking the guesswork out of pricing new bikes. The same goes for parts. Typically the markup for new bikes, parts, and accessories is in the 50 percent range. Thus, you can offer a big sale, perhaps 20 percent off all bikes, from time to time. As for labor in your shop, you can offer basic and advanced tune-ups for flat rates, then charge by the hour plus parts for more complex jobs.

Other Helpful Hints and Advice
Contact an insurance agent to determine the kinds of liability coverage your retail space will need. When you give people a bike for a test ride, make sure that they sign a waiver and wear a helmet.

Many municipalities will require you sell a bike license to each person who buys a new bike. Check with your municipality to find out the license requirements.

Make sure you keep good sales and service records because people may come to you looking for their serial number in the unfortunate event that their bike is stolen.

Consignment Store
- Open a retail store around a particular interest of yours, such as furniture, clothing, or jewelry.
- Sell used items on a consignment basis.

Description

Retail stores stock items they purchase from wholesalers, mark up the prices, and sell them to customers at retail prices. These stores can be focused, such as a women's clothing store, or they can be more general.

Consignment shops offer an alternative to traditional retail stores. *Consignment* refers to items sold on behalf of someone else. In other words, a consignment store does not actually buy products it then sells later. Instead, people bring items in, and if the items fit in with the focus of the store, the consignment shop owner will accept them as part of the store's retail offerings. If the items sell, the people who brought them in make a portion of the sales, and the consignment shop makes a portion of the sales. If the items do not sell, the store owner hasn't lost anything since he or she didn't pay for the items to begin with.

Whatever tangible items you are interested in, you can likely start a consignment shop in that area. Furniture, books, clothing, jewelry, children's toys, sporting goods, and outdoor gear tend to be the most prominent examples of consignment shops, and perhaps the most successful.

Green It!

By their very nature, consignment shops are environmentally friendly. In essence, you are reducing demand for new items by reusing old ones. You are basically extending the useful life of many products. One person's trash is another person's treasure, as the saying goes.

Ecopreneurs in Action

Casey Marsh of The Exchange, a high-end women's consignment shop based in Park City, Utah, started her business in an effort to be green with her career.

Marsh is fully cognizant of the fact that her customers are reusing items rather than buying new, and she has been pleasantly surprised by the quality of items people bring in to sell.

Marsh recently added a book section of the store, to complement her already existing clothing and jewelry offerings, "mainly to keep the men entertained so their wives can shop a little longer," she said with a laugh. Her store is located just off of Main Street in Park City, a very popular pedestrian shopping area, and she indicated that her sign on Main Street is by far her best advertising.

Getting Started

Running a retail store requires great attention to detail, a penchant for interior design, and good organizational skills. Getting a job working in a retail store is easy enough, and it will give you an idea of how to organize products for complementary sales, point-of-sale purchases, and add-ons, all crucial elements of a healthy bottom line.

Start-up costs are much lower for a consignment shop than for a more traditional retail store. In essence, you pay nothing for your entire store's inventory! Until you sell an item, you don't pay for it. This is an enviable position. You will still need to find a space to rent or buy in a good shopping district, a phone system, and a computer and some consignment software to keep track of whose items have sold and whose haven't.

Prevention of theft is always a concern for retail stores, and thus some sort of security system might be in order. Common-sense approaches, like keeping the most expensive items in well-lit, well-trafficked, and easily observed areas (or in the case of jewelry, in a locked glass case) will help you prevent theft.

You will want to have a good contract that states very clearly what yours and your seller's responsibilities are. To get an idea of what this may look like, take a few of your own items to local consignment stores and get copies of their contracts. You'll get a good idea of what considerations the contracts need to have based on a sampling of other consignment stores' contracts so that you can create your own.

Finding Customers

• Location, location, location

Focus on media outlets that cater to whatever it is you're selling. Magazines for professional women might be your best bet if you're focusing on high-end fashion and jewelry, for example. Many customers who bring items in to sell will also be interested in purchasing items in your store. Many times, the items they bring in are in great condition, and they are simply looking to wear a new style or to freshen up their apartment or house with some "new" (new to them) furniture. Thus, make sure you don't disregard these potential clients.

How to Charge

Typically, consignment shops set prices for items as they come in, consulting with the sellers on how much they want. Consignment shops usually take 50 percent of the sale price, so whatever someone wants to make on an item, you'll have to charge double that. If this price turns out to be too high, you'll want to convince the sellers that they need to take less, lest you clog up your retail space with items that just don't sell.

To avoid the clogging issue, you might consider discounting items after they haven't sold for a specific period of time. After one month, you can reduce the overall price on an item that hasn't sold by 15 percent. After two months, reduce it by 30 percent. If it hasn't sold after three months, it's time to get rid of it. You should make sure you have contracts with your sellers stipulating that prices will come down (and the schedule at which they will be discounted). If an item doesn't sell in a specific timeframe, the sellers will have a few days to come pick up the item, after which they will have relinquished the rights to it.

Also stipulate in the contract that it is the seller's responsibility to contact you to see if the item has sold. This way, you don't have to call the sellers all the time to come to your office to pick up their money.

Other Helpful Hints and Advice

You should have some insurance appropriate for running a business in which people will be in your store.

Also, your contract with your sellers should define very clearly how they can go about getting paid for their items.

As your items are reused, you should operate under the *caveat emptor* model: no returns, no exchanges, no guarantees. This relinquishes you of responsibility in the case that someone buys a faulty item, you pay the original seller, and then the buyer returns in a few days to say the item broke. It's unfortunately necessary for this kind of business, and you'll be hard pressed to find a consignment store that operates any other way.

Edible and Organic "Floral" Arrangements

- Use organic fruits to create beautiful and edible alternatives to traditional flower bouquets.
- Use organic flowers to create floral displays that have a more traditional look.

Description

Flowers are traditionally given for a variety of events, holidays, and other occasions in the form of a bouquet or other arrangement. Traditional flowers have a host of environmental problems associated with their production. Freshwater resource consumption is quite high per acre for flower production. Most flowers are grown in chemically intensive ways, in order to create "perfect-looking" flowers. The flower industry is widely accused of unjust working conditions and chronic chemical exposures for its workers. One study found that 60 percent of flower workers have health problems typically associated with chemical exposure, such as neurological damage, cancer, and severe disability (see Organic Consumers Association, www.organicconsumers.org).

Green It!

An alternative floral arrangement consisting entirely of edible (and organic, if possible) accoutrements is a much more environmentally friendly one. It can be made incredibly beautiful, and depending on your artistic abilities, you can create a slew of different kinds of bouquets for various occasions. Use fruits of deep colors (blueberries, strawberries, mango slices, figs, and so on) for more striking arrangements. Use fruits with more bland coloration (bananas, apples, and so on) for more subtle tones and in the background of the deeper colored fruits.

You can either operate this business from a retail store, with or without delivery, or you can run it from your home by delivering all the orders. If you choose to make deliveries, consider using a biofuel-powered vehicle (any diesel vehicle can use biodiesel; check out www.biodiesel.org for fuel availability in your area).

The disadvantage of this business is that your arrangements are going to cost more than traditional flowers. If, for example, you are using organic blueberries, you will have to use them sparingly or your arrangement may cost you $20 simply for the fruit! To save money, you can sometimes get large bags of frozen fruit, like blueberries and strawberries, on sale during the growing season. Save these and use them throughout the rest of the year rather than continuously buying fresh fruit. Keeping staple items like frozen blueberries and strawberries around will also help you to "whip up" a quick arrangement on short notice, should the need arise. Frozen fruit will also help keep your edible bouquets cold and fresh during delivery.

Currently, companies selling edible bouquets are charging up to $55 for bouquet-sized arrangements. Customers are proving willing to pay the price because the bouquet serves not only for beauty but for a snack at the reception. A few extra dollars to make the arrangements organic will not make or break the sale, especially for LOHAS consumers, who will appreciate that the fruit is organic.

If you are thinking of using organically grown flowers, check your local area for growers of organic flowers. If you can be assured of a steady supply, an organic florist shop is also a great business to run. Watch out for hydroponically grown flowers, especially roses, as these tend to have greater numbers of thorns than sun-grown flowers.

Getting Started

You will need to find some serving baskets, preferably of a sustainable material like woven bamboo, that are inexpensive yet attractive. They will need to be deep enough to hold a layer of fruit but not so deep that it will cost you twice as much to fill as you will charge. Experiment with a few types of baskets, see what it costs to fill them, how long it takes you, and how much competitors (if there are any edible bouquet companies nearby) are charging for similar crafts.

If you decide to open a retail store, it need not be big. Think in terms of ice cream parlors. People can walk along your cooler case, examine a few different artistically created arrangements, and pick the one they want.

If you decide to offer delivery services, you will need a way to get your arrangements to a location. Choose a fuel-efficient hybrid or a vehicle that can run on biofuels like biodiesel. This not only makes environmental sense but also makes good business sense, saving you money on fuel as gas prices go up and up and ...

Finding Customers

- Flyers
  - Health food stores
  - Vegetarian restaurants
- Media outlets including those for niche markets
  - Local health and environmentally themed monthly magazines
  - Coupons and coupon books
- Booths
  - Home and garden shows
  - Farmers' markets

Make sure your advertising materials are professional and very attractive because your arrangements will sell at least partially based on the merits of their appearance. Use color in your print advertising.

You can also do some indirect marketing by donating arrangements to local environmental nonprofit groups during their annual benefits and silent auctions.

You can also try to sell your goods through retail outlets like health food stores and local florists. This may yet be the best outlet for your goods because you will be able to focus on production and leave the marketing to the retailers, but it also will require you to give a significant portion of your profits to them.

How to Charge

Once you've found a decent basket and made a handful of arrangements, you will have a good idea of how much it costs you to create each one. You'll need to mark your price up significantly to cover costs of distribution, marketing, spoilage, irregular demand, and other unforeseen expenses. You can start with a 50 percent markup and then adjust it as you see fit.

You can give bulk discounts to retail outlets that are selling your goods. They provide a terrific service to you in terms of distribution, promotion, and volume sales. Thus, a healthy cut should go to them. If you are unsure of how much of a cut to give them, ask them to suggest a cut, and then negotiate from there.

Make sure you're making a margin significant enough to support your operations and to cover any unexpected costs, such as food spoilage or package damage.

Until you are up and running smoothly, you may expect to lose 10 to 20 percent of your packages to spoilage. While this is unfortunate, it is part of the business, and you may have to just chalk it up to experience. Hopefully, in the long run, you will become greatly more efficient and prosperous.

Other Helpful Hints and Advice

Make sure you have checked with your state and/or local municipality regarding a food handler's permit. Also, put expiration dates on all arrangements. If you have someone making deliveries for you, make sure that person is insured in the event of an accident. Remember also to consider food allergies, warnings of choking hazards, and the like.

Green Building Supply Store

- Open a retail store and stock environmentally friendly building materials.
- Consult for architects, planners, designers, and homeowners on health and environmental concerns throughout the building or remodeling process.

Description

Building supply stores are big business. The Home Depot and Lowe's are the biggest, but there are also smaller chains like Ace Hardware, Standard Builders, and Industrial Supply. These stores stock essentially everything a homeowner or a builder would need to build or remodel a building and landscape the surrounding land.

Green It!

Green building supply centers have opened in a selection of cities across America in recent years. (For an in-depth description of what green building is, visit the U.S. Green Building Council Web site at www.usgbc.org.) This market is steadily growing because of the public's deepening concerns over energy efficiency, the harvesting of old growth forests, other resource utilization and depletion issues, and health concerns related to the chemicals used in the traditional manufacturing of paints, sealants, plasters, and many other building products.

Green building supply stores carry alternative products that are both environmentally friendly and healthier for a building's occupants. Wholesale companies like EcoTimber (sustainable hardwoods and other ecofriendly flooring products: www. ecotimber.com) and American Pride (nontoxic paints made without petrochemical ingredients: www.americanpridepaint. com) have made the retail side of this business easier for someone looking to open a green building supply store. For most building products, there is an environmentally friendly alternative.

Opening a green building supply store in your town will create a whirlwind of attention in the building community. Everyone from architects and landscape designers on down to painting subcontractors will come out of the woodwork to get on board the green building revolution. For many of these folks, a desire to be a part of the industry arises from genuine concern over issues like tropical forest degradation or chronic exposure to petrochemical-laden products. For others, it is more motivated by a desire to be part of a rapidly growing and high-end industry.

In terms of competition, green building supply stores cannot compete directly with The Home Depot and Lowe's. Prices for green products will be higher that they are for similar products (like recycled glass tiles versus traditional ceramic tiles), and your selection will likely be much smaller than that of a Big Box competitor. But cost is not how a green building supply store will compete with the Big Box stores. By nature, the green building supply store provides a niche market for a health- and environment-conscious clientele interested in sustainable and, at the same time, attractive products.

In the meantime, you get to advocate for more energy-efficient buildings and make money doing so. You can sell recycled cotton or wool insulation, drip irrigation systems to encourage Xeriscaping, tankless hot water heaters, radiant floor heating systems, solar photovoltaic systems, solar hot water systems, swamp coolers, and triple paned and other high-efficiency windows. To replace the demand for petrochemical-based products, you can sell green products such as nontoxic paints, plasters, and sealants; organic fertilizers; and nontoxic weed and feed compounds. You can also carry sustainably harvested products, such as bamboo, cork, FSC certified hardwoods, straw bale, and insulated concrete forms for building foundations.

As mentioned earlier in the "House and Office Services" entry, the Forest Stewardship Council (FSC) is an independent organization that certifies sustainable harvest practices in the timber industry. You can trust that anything with an FSC certification is made from wood that was harvested sustainably (for example, in patch cuts versus clear cuts or from young forests rather than old growth or other sensitive forest ecosystems). There is a similar organization called the Sustainable Forest Initiative (SFI). However, the SFI is industry based, and its standards are only slightly better than business as usual and fall quite a bit short of the standards set by the FSC.

Ecopreneurs in Action

Ashley Patterson started the Green Building Center in 2003. Her store is a model of green building products, allowing customers to see a variety of sustainable flooring products, healthy paints and plasters, and a solar photovoltaic array on her roof. The best part of the business, she says, is "meeting the coolest people in the area." She sees the green building industry growing exponentially: "As more [green building supply] stores open up across the country, I think the network of green building centers will become a force to be reckoned with." This should make sustainable building products ever more popular in the mainstream consciousness.

Getting Started

A background in green building or design will be instrumental in helping you to sell products that are relatively new to many home-owners and contractors. You will have to do a lot of consulting, helping people get their projects going and instructing them on the use of particular products.

Educational seminars on green building are going on around the country and throughout the year; you may want to attend several of these before committing to opening a store.

To learn more, there are also great books on green building, and the U.S. Green Building Council (GBC) is a valuable resource as well.

Be absolutely positive you know the true green products from the "greenwashed" items (for example, the FSC versus the SFI certifications for sustainable forestry).

Experience in managing a retail store will give you an idea of how to organize products for marketing and selling complemen-tary items; how to set up point-of-sale purchase systems; how to run seasonal sales and offer bulk and contractor discounts; and how to increase profit margins using sales add-ons—all crucial elements of maintaining a healthy bottom line.

Your retail store itself and its inventory will be the most significant elements in your start-up capital. This is an expensive business to start, but the potential rewards from it are better than those of many other green businesses.

Finding Customers

- Location, location, location
- Flyers
  - Naturopathic physicians' offices
- Media outlets including those for niche markets
  - Local health and environmentally themed monthly magazines
  - National Public Radio
- Booths
  - Home and garden shows
- Press releases

Green building supply stores often benefit greatly from being positioned near Big Box home improvement centers, which are usually "anchors" for all sorts of other specialty building supply stores. Employees of the Big Box stores often send a great deal of business to surrounding stores when their stores do not have particular specialty items customers are looking for. Make sure the employees in the nearby Big Box stores know what your store offers in case they have customers looking for the kinds of products you are selling. It is also far more convenient for contractors (who will make up a large contingent of your steady customers) to go to one district to obtain all the supplies they need for a particular job.

You should also do some direct marketing with green architects and contractors in town, people with whom you can likely send business back and forth. One green building store owner stated that "Lunch and Learn" sessions with local architects were her best marketing methods. You should offer contractors a discount, perhaps 10 percent.

Offer classes to help bring people into the store. To help you organize and publicize these classes, consider partnering with other organizations—for example, work with the local utility companies to develop energy efficiency programs or work with the local non-profit organizations that promote solar panel installations and other clean and renewable energy projects for homeowners and businesses. Some of the companies that make green products might be interested to help you organize and run classes on their building products such as natural paints and plasters.

Organize a local green home tour. People who own green homes tend to be proud of them and therefore willing to show them. This will allow people who are curious about the industry to see a finished project and decide whether they could remodel their house in the same way.

How to Charge

Manufacturers have a suggested retail price (MSRP) for their products. This helps make your pricing job less difficult, but there is still significant flexibility in what you actually decide to charge. For example, you may decide to sell some items at cost in order to bring people in, in hopes that you will be able to sell them other complementary items at the same time. You may also have a passion about certain items, and you may decide to keep your margins very low on those items so that you may sell more of them. It's all up to you.

If you are offering consulting services, make sure to charge a fee significant enough to make the consultation worth your time. Let customers know up front what your consulting fees are, or else risk having your time and expertise abused by well-meaning customers. Let them know that you'd be happy to help them but you are incredibly busy running your store and therefore you need to charge for your time. If, however, your customer is buying a large amount of a product and simply needs to know how to use it, you can certainly offer to help him or her for an hour free of charge. Define your boundaries, thus letting customers know that your time and expertise are valuable things.

Other Helpful Hints and Advice

Insure your store against liability, and your inventory against theft, fire, and so on. Most of your wholesalers will guarantee their products, meaning that if a customer is not happy with the outcome, you will be able to replace or refund the purchase through the wholesaler.

. . . .

Green Product Retail Store

- Open a retail store and stock items of environmental, Fair Trade, and health orientation.

Description

Retail stores are the quintessential Mom & Pop business in American folklore. One of the first things people think of when they want to start a business is to "open a little store specializing in...." Retail stores tend to be subject to intense competition. Many communities lament the loss of their Mom & Pop businesses when Big Box generalist stores come to town. Thus, most successful new retail stores tend to focus exclusively on a niche market to avoid direct competition with Big Box rivals.

Green It!

A store specifically devoted to environmentally friendly goods can carry a wide variety of items, including organic cotton clothing, bamboo furniture, energy-efficient lights, bicycle commuter gear, rechargeable batteries, gifts made from recycled glass, hemp jewelry, and a great deal more. The store will be limited more by space constraints and other practical concerns than by a lack of green products to fill it.

An alternative type of environmentally friendly retail store is known as a Fair Trade retail store. Fair Trade shops sell goods imported from emerging-economy countries. In these developing countries, most workers are typically paid very little and subjected to substandard working conditions. In contrast, workers protected under Fair Trade agreements are guaranteed a living wage and good working conditions. In addition, Fair Trade companies avoid employing child labor and operating sweatshops.

The advantage to running a green product retail store is that competition with the Big Box stores, which can usually beat any small retail outlet on price, will be fairly minimal. The obvious disadvantage is that many green and Fair Trade certified products aren't necessarily daily necessities, and thus you are dependent on your customers' discretionary spending for the majority of your sales.

Ecopreneurs in Action

Scott Lowe of Ten Thousand Villages likes the idea of changing the economic conditions that have led to so much environmental and social degradation. What he finds most inspiring about his store is the difference he sees in the customers themselves. "We see the people that come in the store on a regular basis and those that come in the first time, and it is quite a difference," he says. "Most are excited to know how they can play their part in promoting fair trade and sustainable economic growth."

Thom Benedict of Earth Goods General Store advises that if people wish to begin an eco-friendly product store, they should "start small and grow from there." Benedict's store carries products as diverse as organic cotton and alternative fiber clothing, recycled paper office supplies, and bulk, refillable liquid laundry soap.

Developing a product line is quite challenging, he says, but it is one of the really fun parts of the business. He says that location is very important and that you need to make your margins on items that are not easy to find in other stores—you can't charge much of a premium for organic lip balm, for example, since it can be found fairly cheaply at natural food stores, but you can charge a slightly better margin for organic cotton clothing because that item is not as readily available.

Benedict says that his best advertising comes from radio ads, especially National Public Radio (NPR): "Radio tends to be more interactive than print media. People who come in from radio ads are excited about the store already, whereas with print media, I feel like they are coming in to kick the tires a bit."

Getting Started

Being able to talk intelligently about different environmental or social justice issues will give you the ability to sell products related to addressing those issues. It will also prevent you from stocking your store with anything but the most authentic of the green and Fair Trade certified products.

Running a retail store requires great attention to detail, an eye for interior design, and good organizational skills. Getting a job working in a retail store is easy enough, and it will give you ideas for how to organize products for complementary sales, point-of-sale purchases, and add-ons.

Start-up costs will depend on what kinds of products you want to fill your store with, whether you rent or buy your retail space, and how much square footage you have decided to have.

Prevention of theft is always a concern for retail stores, and thus some sort of security system might be in order. Common-sense precautions, like keeping the most expensive items in well-lit, well-trafficked, and easily observed areas (or in the case of jewelry, in locked glass cases), will help you prevent theft.

Finding Customers
- Location, location, location
- Flyers
  - Vegetarian restaurants
  - Coffee shops
  - Outdoor gear retailers
- Media outlets including those for niche markets
  - Local health and environmentally themed monthly magazines
  - National Public Radio
  - Coupons and coupon books
- Networking
  - Green Drinks
- Press releases

How to Charge
Manufacturers have a suggested retail price (MSRP) for their products. This helps make your pricing job less difficult, but there is still significant flexibility in what you actually decide to charge. For example, you may decide to sell some items at cost in order to bring people in, in hopes that you will be able to sell them other complementary items at the same time. You may also have a passion about certain items, and you may decide to keep your margins very low on those items so that you may sell more of them. It's all up to you.

Team Opportunities
While it is a nonprofit, an individual can start a Ten Thousand Villages store by forming a local nonprofit organization [in the United States, it would be set up with the Internal Revenue Service as a 501(c) (3) tax-exempt organization]. Besides the nonprofit status and disbursement of net income, there is little difference in running a store like this versus a for-profit retail store. For more information, visit www.tenthousandvillages.com/php/about.us/start.a.store.php.

Native and Organic Plant Nursery

- Propagate, grow, and sell plants for landscape and garden applications.
- Specialize in native plants that have adapted naturally to the local climatic conditions.
- Offer food-producing trees and other plants grown from organic seed.
- Consult with homeowners on how they can place trees and shrubs as a way of cutting energy bills.
- Sell biological agents for pest control (for example, ladybugs and praying mantis), organic fertilizers, and other ecofriendly gardening alternatives.

Description

Plant nurseries grow and sell plants for landscape and garden applications. Retail nurseries buy plants from wholesale nurseries or other growers and sell them to the general public. Wholesalers usually specialize in the propagation of plants for sale to the retail outlets and commercial landscaping companies. Nurseries may also sell gardening tools, equipment, and supplies, including compost, topsoil, bark mulch, fertilizer, and weed and pest control products.

Green It!

Native plants are adapted to the local climatic conditions. This means that native plants typically need less fertilizer, pesticide, water, maintenance, and other upkeep than nonnative plants, and they are typically more resistant to pests and local climatic extremes that often require the use of chemicals. Thus, a nursery that specializes in native plants will help homeowners and businesses to use less chemical pesticide and fertilizer in their landscapes. Those landscapes will likely require less water as well.

Food-bearing plants will allow homeowners to harvest from their gardens, reducing the need for food grown in other parts of the world to be shipped to their supermarkets. These can be anything from annual veggies to perennial fruit-bearing trees.

Deciduous trees (for example, maples, oaks, and most fruit trees) can provide shade in the summer and allow the sun to warm a building in the winter. Evergreen trees provide not only shade but can also be effective wind-blockers for cold wintry gusts that strip a home's heat. Planting evergreen trees on the side of the building that takes the brunt of most of the winter storm systems may help cut heating bills significantly.

Ecopreneurs in Action

Gayle Weyher of Grow Wild Nursery saw a lot of waste in the landscaping industry in Utah, a desert state. She saw a need for more native, drought-tolerant plants both for the general public and for professional landscapers. Grow Wild sells mostly Utah native plants, but it also sells a few drought-tolerant varieties from other areas and some food-producing plants, such as berry bushes and fruit trees.

Getting Started

Having a degree in horticulture certainly helps you run a nursery, but it is by no means necessary as long as you know your plants and gardening. You can gain a great deal of experience working in a local nursery for a little while before striking off on your own. You will learn installation and maintenance of drip irrigation systems, elements of shading, and other details of growing (and keeping alive) potted plants. Shading and other shelter are particularly important because a very hot day can ruin many plants, as can a storm with powerful winds and rain or a frost.

Your choice of retail location is less important than it would be in other retail settings because people often make special trips to buy lots of plants all at once. Keep in mind that you'll need a convenient area where trucks and vehicles with trailers can load plants and other landscaping materials.

You will need to have a property on which customers can peruse your goods.

You will need compost (get it delivered in bulk), fertilizer (organic ones are fairly widespread), a large quantity of pots (there are biodegradable pots that you can put directly into the ground), and a variety of shovels, picks, hoses and other garden supplies. A greenhouse, even a homemade variety, will help you get a head start on spring so that your plants will be ready to sell when people are just starting to think about planting.

One of the main challenges of running a nursery is its seasonal nature. Spring and fall are going to be quite busy, as these are typically the best planting seasons. Business will be a little slower in the summer and nonexistent in the winter if you live in a climate with freezing winter temperatures.

Finding Customers

- Direct sales
- Media outlets including those for niche markets
  - Local health and environmentally themed monthly magazines
- Booths
  - Home and garden shows
  - Farmers' markets
- Press releases

Landscaping companies tend to patronize wholesale nurseries for lower prices and bulk discounts, but they need items from time to time from retail nurseries geographically closest to their job sites. Either way you choose to run your nursery, pick up the phone book and call all the landscaping companies in it to let them know of your selection and location. If you have a flyer, ask the companies if you can mail them copies of it. Especially focus on landscaping companies that advertise in green business directories, natural health publications, and the like because they may do more business in native plants than other landscaping companies. Any advertising you do should coincide with your region's warm seasons because this business will be seasonal. Thus, monthly magazines may be better than annual phone books.

How to Charge

Look around at other nurseries in your area to gauge their prices. Buying from a wholesale nursery, you will likely have to mark your prices up 50 to 100 percent in order to cover the losses from plants that don't survive or don't sell.

If you decide to open a wholesale nursery, consider that retailers and landscaper contractors will buy in bulk from you and thus expect very low prices per plant. Look around at retail nurseries in your area to gauge their prices. Typically, they will mark up your products 50 to 100 percent over what you are charging them, so if you see a retail nursery selling a six-inch acorn squash for $4.99, you will likely have to sell it to them for $2.50.

Other Helpful Hints and Advice

Contact an insurance agent to find out about the extent of your liabilities, and use common sense (such as putting up "wet floor" signs around the area you are watering). If any of your plants have significant thorns, allergy-inducing pollens, or other bothersome features, clearly label them as such. Some nurseries guarantee their plants for one season, though this is a risky policy and not usually necessary.

Printer Cartridge Refilling Store

• Open a retail store that refills ink cartridges from printers.

Description

Everyone who owns a printer for his or her computer, digital camera, or other electronic device has to keep it stocked with fresh ink and toner cartridges, and the average household has at least two printers. Printer manufacturers are decreasing the volume of ink or toner in cartridges with each new generation of printers to hit the market. Some cartridges must be replaced on a weekly basis, depending on use.

It may seem like a small thing, but the statistics are somewhat staggering on printer cartridge disposal. It takes approximately one gallon of oil to create a new printer cartridge. According to information on the Web site www.cartridgeworld.com, about 350 million inkjet cartridges are thrown away in North America every year. Worldwide, enough cartridges are thrown away every year to circle the entire earth three times if stacked end to end. Petrochemical-based ingredients in these cartridges will take over a thousand years to degrade.

In addition, refilling cartridges locally creates jobs in your area and reduces transportation costs (and pollution) by reducing demand for products that need to be shipped from overseas.

Green It!

A retail store that specializes in recycling (in industry lingo, it is called "remanufacturing") empty printer cartridges will help save consumers money and reduce needless waste. You will not only be providing an environmental service but customers will also save money over the cost of buying a new printer cartridge. Often the savings can be substantial, in the neighborhood of 50 percent off on many products.

Ecopreneurs in Action

Jennifer Schaerer chose to start a Cartridge World in Draper, Utah, because of her growing concern about our "throwaway" culture. She said, "We've always thought that we're so incredibly wasteful [in America], that all this beautiful space will be filled with landfills unless we do something about it." There are a number of inkjet refilling retail operations, but Cartridge World stood out to Schaerer for a number of reasons: "We chose the market leader for the branding that came along with it. People know Cartridge World is the most established in the industry, and there's a quality inherent in the business. Cartridge World also takes a whole-business approach to being environmentally friendly. For example, the suppliers of our business have chosen to take an environmental tract with their business operations in order to do business with us."

Getting Started

Previous knowledge of the computing and printing industries is a benefit in beginning a store devoted to the remanufacture of printer cartridges. Familiarity with all the different kinds of printing equipment commonly used in home and office settings will prove quite helpful in speaking intelligently with your customers.

A retail location is needed, though it doesn't need to be anything large or fancy because your product offerings will be fairly limited and your inventory pretty insignificant. Most stores of this kind sell a variety of remanufactured printer cartridges (commonly used cartridges should be ready and available when a customer walks in the door, while rarely used cartridges can be refilled when the customers bring them in); printer paper; some flash drives and other storage devices; and other computer support hardware.

The equipment necessary to refill a wide variety of printer cartridges can be purchased from wholesalers of this kind of equipment, who will provide a user's manual and perhaps some training. You may need a handful of employees to cover all the store hours, or to be refilling cartridges in the back while you are helping customers. You will also want to have gloves and perhaps respiratory masks for you and your employees while you are working in the lab in the back of the store.

Finding Customers

- Direct sales
- Media outlets including those for niche markets
  - Coupons and coupon books

Partnerships with local nonprofit organizations, by which you pay them for each printer cartridge they bring in, will help you get the word out about your environmental commitment and create a sense of goodwill among your customers. Use direct sales methods to reach local businesses because they may be high-end customers that are more sophisticated than the general public.

How to Charge

You'll be able to surmise your costs for remanufacturing a printer cartridge, including the time it takes you to refill it, the ink, and the cost of the refilling machine itself, amortized over the life of the equipment. Give yourself a considerable markup, and then compare that price to the retail price of new cartridges and to those of your other competitor remanufacturers in the area, if there are any. You will likely see that you can make good margins, yet still save your customers a considerable amount over the purchase of new cartridges. It is advised to keep your costs about 40 percent below what it costs to buy a new cartridge. Remember that coupons may be your best advertising, at least in reaching new customers for the first time, so you have to have enough of a margin to cover any further discounts you give out in that way.

Other Helpful Hints and Advice

You should have insurance appropriate for running a business in which people will be in your store. You will also want to find out about any safety issues related to your remanufacturing machines from the distributor of that machine, and act accordingly to protect you, your employees, and your customers.

Team Opportunities

Cartridge World, a global leader in remanufactured inkjet cartridges and other printing services, offers franchises in many countries. At time this book went to press, there were approximately 1,500 Cartridge World stores globally. See www.cartridge-world.com for more information.

....

Used-Book Exchange

- Open a retail store buying, selling, and trading used books.
- Provide regular customers a credit program, encouraging significant reuse of books.

Description

Bookstores buy books wholesale from publishers or their agents and then sell them direct to the public with a fairly significant markup. Bookstores often sell calendars, gifts, board games, and a variety of related items, and sometimes they even contain a small coffee bar so that customers may sit and browse a few books before deciding on one. In recent years, bigger bookstore chains have overtaken most small, independent bookstores because the chain stores can take advantage of economies of scale, they can stock a greater variety of books and other merchandise, and they have bigger advertising budgets. Niche-market bookstores, such as those that sell used books, may be able to resist competition from larger chain bookstores simply by offering a very different service.

Green It!

Not only does selling used books create an economic opportunity for an aspiring entrepreneur, it is also an environmentally superior alternative to selling new books. Buying people's used books keeps those books from collecting dust on a bookshelf, going to the landfill, or being recycled without reuse. Another excellent opportunity for environmental activism by a used-book exchange is to make up a prominent display rack of books on environmental topics (like this one!). You can create this display table or bookshelf right at the entrance to the store or right by the cash register, where just about every customer will see them.

Ecopreneurs in Action

Pam Pedersen of the Central Book Exchange feels very good about her green business. "Everything is 100 percent recycled here," she says. "If a book comes in and it doesn't sell, we give it to a company that shreds it and makes attic insulation out of it." As a low-budget operation, she says that affording advertising is the hardest part of the business, but "there are a lot of people who are concerned and curious that we are doing well, and they are supporting us."

Getting Started

Start by collecting as many used books in excellent to good condition as you can through friends, yard sales, your own collection, or at public library book sales. Focus on books in terrific condition, as well as books by well-known authors that will most likely sell quickly. Don't be afraid to turn away a lot of books that are in moderate or outright bad condition or that are not by popular authors.

You'll need a decent retail location, preferably in a walkable commercial district or neighborhood. It doesn't need to be large, but it has to have enough space for a good selection of books and for people to browse without feeling cramped. If you can provide a few sitting areas, and perhaps a coffee bar, customers will feel comfortable and will tend to purchase more (this will also act as an additional revenue stream). You may choose to contact a coffee roaster or wholesaler that is interested in having a retail location and just rent some space to that company rather than doing it yourself. Consider organic, shade grown, and Fair Trade coffees (triple certified).

There are many software packages on the market that will help you keep track of your inventory. You can shop online for these. Keep in mind that you will want a scanner to read the ISBN codes on the back of the books, in order to quickly and efficiently manage your inventory.

To keep track of your credit program with customers, a simple Excel spreadsheet should do the trick. These spreadsheets can be alphabetized by the customer's last name so that you can quickly look up someone's information. Your program for trade should allow people to bring used books in, donate them, and get credits toward new purchases. Most book exchanges might offer partial credit and partial cash purchases of books, so that if a customer has brought in a couple of books, he or she should have sufficient credit to make their next purchase very inexpensive.

Finding Customers
- Location, location, location
- Flyers
  - Coffee shops
  - Outdoor gear retailers
- Media outlets including those for niche markets
  - Coupons and coupon books

You can also do book readings, signings with authors, acoustic music, poetry readings, and other events that bring people in. The book exchange would not be complete, of course, without a customer loyalty program. You can offer a trade-in value that is more than the cash you would pay for a used book. This encourages people to put their money back into your store and it also increases their loyalty to your store.

How to Charge

You can mark up your books significantly from what you pay for them. Most people will sell their used books for pennies on the dollar, and even if you mark them up to half of their original retail price (which may be 8 to 10 times more than you paid for them), you will still be significantly undercutting the price someone would have to pay for the books if they were new. You may choose to offer someone 3 times as much value in trade-in as they get in cash for their used books.

Other Helpful Hints and Advice

You should have some insurance appropriate for running a business in which people will be in your store. Because your items are reused, you should offer no returns, no exchanges, and no guarantees. This policy protects you in the event that someone buys a faulty item for which you have already paid the seller, then returns in a few days to say the book is missing page 121. A no-return policy is unfortunately necessary for this kind of business, and you'll be hard pressed to find a store selling used items that operates any other way.

Services to Businesses and Nonprofit Organizations

- Fundraiser and/or Grant Writer
- Independent Publicist
- Independent Sales Representative
- Restaurant Delivery Service
- Specialty Advertising
- Sustainability Consultant

Fundraiser and Grant Writer

- Call existing and potential donors to request funds for an environmental nonprofit organization or one of its projects.
- Get creative with silent auctions, event sponsorships, car washes, bake sales, and any other way you can get funding for your organization while simultaneously increasing its public presence.
- Write grant proposals to help fund environmental groups, events, or businesses.

Description

Local nonprofit organizations sometimes hire fundraisers and grant writers to help them raise funds during a crucial time in their operations. Typically, these fundraisers and grant writers have grant writing and sales experience and can exceed the fundraising objectives of the organization, which means they can take out their fees from the funds they raise that are over the amount the nonprofit needs. Thus, they can pay for themselves and in the process free up the time of the nonprofit's employees to concentrate on science, policy, or whatever else it is that is their specialty. A grant writer will send out proposals to various funding organizations (including governmental organizations and foundations) to secure funding mainly for nonprofit groups, scientific expeditions, and, increasingly, the private sector.

Green It!

Lend your skills to environmental nonprofit organizations and green businesses to help them secure funding for various projects.

Getting Started

Sales experience is useful. You should have the ability to convey ideas and excitement over the phone and through writing. Groups will likely want you to call their list of current and former members, introduce whatever project they are looking to raise money for, and then ask for the members' financial or in-kind support.

Grant writing is a different fundraising avenue. There are grant writing workshops offered by many community education schools. The true education for this field, however, comes in the experience itself. Accumulate a list of agencies and foundations that give grants in the area you are interested working in and their requirements for grant applications. The U.S. Environmental Protection Agency and the U.S. Department of Energy, for example, frequently give grants to businesses that are developing renewable and domestic energy projects.

Your start-up costs are negligible. You'll need a computer and the ability to do a great deal of research (a public library or a local university library, if you have access to one).

Finding Customers

- Direct sales
- Web
  - Facebook
- Networking
  - Green Drinks
  - Drinking Liberally
  - EarthSave.org
  - Sierra Club groups
  - Outdoors clubs

Focus your direct sales efforts on all the local environmental non-profit organizations, local green businesses, and larger businesses that have green projects.

How to Charge

Some organizations that have hired fundraisers before will have a set schedule of what they pay fundraisers. It may be a flat fee, but more than likely it will be a certain percentage of the money you raise. Starting off, you may want to ask for 15 percent. As you get more experience and your business grows, you may ask for a higher percentage. Don't be afraid to negotiate. Another key component to your fee scale is whether you will have access to the group's existing donor list. If you have to find donors yourself, you can charge substantially more for your services than if you're given a member list to work with.

For grants, you may also ask a certain percentage of the total award amount. If you don't know what to charge, simply ask your potential clients what they would consider paying you for a successful grant.

Other Helpful Hints and Advice

There are few significant legal or insurance issues to consider, as long as you play by the rules of both your client and funding agency.

Independent Publicist

- Help your clients get free press by appearing in TV or radio talk shows, in articles in print and online newspapers and other media, and at public gatherings.
- Focus your expertise in the growing sustainable economy, and specialize in promoting green companies and nonprofit organizations.

Description

A good publicist will help companies promote their products or services without spending a lot of money on advertising. To generate "buzz" for a company, a publicist will use his or her contacts in the media (TV, radio, newspapers, or other periodicals) and creativity to get people talking about a particular business. Publicists work to get their clients onto talk shows and to send out press releases when appropriate. If it's a slow news day, the newspaper might just pick up the story and run with it. In this way, publicists can generate a different kind of publicity than traditional advertising. People tend to react more positively toward the company being promoted in the context of a news story than a simple print ad.

Green It!

You can become a green publicist by working with environmentally friendly businesses in your area. Work hard to promote them as the "new face of business," where the 1970s era environmentalism meets modern market efficiency. There has been a surge of interest in the burgeoning sustainable economy, and the media are looking to publish feel-good stories of businesses doing well by doing the right thing, so selling publicity should not be difficult. For clients, you can also work to promote environmental nonprofits, authors of books about environmental issues, or public speakers in the fields of the environment, green business, or natural health and wellness.

Ecopreneurs in Action

Michael Straus of Straus Communications started promoting his family's organic dairy, Straus Family Creamery, and he realized that he could use his expertise in the organic agriculture industry to help other green companies. By publicizing organic agricultural methods, Straus has earned a reputation as a knowledgeable expert in a rapidly growing industry, which has given him access to editors, reporters, and other media that frequently need information about subjects like organics and sustainability. This, in turn, has given Straus the ability to publicize businesses and causes that he represents through these media connections, resulting in win-win situations for all parties. If you want to get into the PR business for green companies, Straus recommends, "Be really clear that this is what you want to do, and be flexible as the business evolves to change course if necessary." For more information, see www.strauscom.com.

Getting Started

Experience in marketing, advertising sales, or promotions would be very helpful. Good contacts in the media are tantamount. Learn who the important people are and who might be sympathetic to your cause. Do this by identifying local radio DJs who frequently speak about environmental issues, reading the newspaper and identifying the writers who tend to write about these issues, and surveying other local publications for guest writers interested in environmental topics.

If you charge creatively based on success only (as suggested on page 196 in "How to Charge"), you might find clients more willing to sign up. Pick businesses you truly believe in and get started by representing them. Feel free to ask them if they want more than just the occasional attempt at free press—you may just find a great client who has his or her own ideas on marketing but has no time to follow up.

Finding Customers
- Direct sales
- Networking
  - EarthSave.org
  - Sierra Club groups

Focus your direct sales on any green businesses and nonprofits in your area, and network within the green community persistently.

How to Charge
Typically a publicist will charge by a set period of time, whether it is by the hour for consulting work or by the month for ongoing projects. To get an idea of the going rate, you can call other publicists in town and ask about their rates and fee structures.

An interesting alternative is to charge through results only. Sign on a client, letting him or her know that you'll be working concurrently on a variety of promotions and that you will charge him or her only if you're able to get him or her a radio interview, or a front page story, or whatever the measure of success.

Other Helpful Hints and Advice
There are few legal or insurance issues, and very little liability, as you will mostly be operating behind the scenes. However, it is recommended that you have good legal counsel available and strong contracts that can be easily and clearly negotiated.

Independent Sales Representative
- Represent environmentally friendly products or services to a target market by making sales calls and providing distribution support if necessary.

- Visit retailers with product samples, and attempt to convince them to carry the products you represent.

Description

A lot has changed since Willy Loman's days as the lead character in *Death of a Salesman*. Then again, a lot remains exactly the same. Technology and a never-ending quest for speed and efficiency in business have led to some great advances for salespeople in terms of how they can showcase a product or service. Most good salespeople will tell you, however, that the most important parts of a job in sales are still pounding the pavement, knocking on doors, and having a firm handshake and a confident smile.

Green It!

Sell something green! There are thousands of environmentally friendly products you can represent, from sustainably harvested hardwood floors (for example, see www.ecotimber.com) to home solar and wind power products to organic, shade grown, and Fair Trade certified coffees (for example, see www.caffeibis.com).

Your advantage is that you're passionate and knowledgeable about your products, which are key components of any good salesperson's success. Your timing is also quite good, as more and more businesses and individuals are "going green" with their purchases. Your products may cost a bit more than their generic competitors, but if you're a good salesperson, you'll find a way to turn that disadvantage into an advantage (for example, tell restaurateurs that they can charge more for the premium organic lettuce, or say to them, "Yes, but who would want *generic iceberg lettuce*?! It's so *blah!*").

Getting Started

A company has to invest time, money, and other resources in training and supporting its salespeople. In order to justify that expenditure, that company has to believe in you and your ability to work independently. In other words, you may have to sell them on you and your company!

There are virtually no start-up costs for the business as long as you have decent clothes, a laptop computer, a phone, and a way to get from place to place in a timely fashion.

Finding a product to sell is simple. If you have any expertise in a particular area, and you want to see more green products in that area enter the marketplace, find those green products you believe in, and go contact their companies to see if they need any independent salespeople.

For example, if you want to support local organic farmers, find as many as possible, and one by one, contact them to see if they would like you to represent their products. You will bring information about their products, including price, distribution, and promotions, to restaurateurs or grocers, trying to convince those people to carry the products you represent. Restaurateurs and small independent grocers are among the busiest people you will ever meet, and if they can meet with one sales representative who represents multiple natural food items, you may find that they will buy everything from you and be done meeting with other salespeople.

In one fell swoop, you will "green up" a restaurant's menu, you will make several sales that will continue to pay you a commission for as long as the restaurant continues to serve those products, and you will make your clients very happy.

Finding Customers
- Direct sales

Contact wholesalers of interest to see if they are looking for salespeople and/or distributors of their goods. Once you are representing a line of goods, you can then begin contacting retailers that may be interested in carrying those products.

How to Charge
Set up a system with the companies who are hiring your business to sell their products. You can go on commission only: if you sell

a product that the customer continues to buy, say, a coffee shop to which you sell a triple certified coffee, you can ask for a residual commission as long as that coffee shop continues to serve that coffee. This way, the coffee wholesaler gets a great sale, and as long as you did your job well, you make a great (and continuing) commission that will hopefully last for a very long time.

You can also charge a flat fee for representing a client's products, but where's the fun in that?

Other Helpful Hints and Advice

Make sure you have contracts with both the companies you are representing and with the customers you are selling to. Make sure the contract designates you as a third-party representative for the company you are selling for, not a party who is responsible for product quality. Make sure you can incorporate a continuing commission as long as the retailers continue to carry your wholesaler's products. This will protect you from being excluded and assures that everyone involved is interested in thinking about each other's best interests for the long term.

You can set up your company as an independent contractor hired by the companies you are representing—it's a tax advantage for them, and it may help convince them that you have their best interests in mind. An attorney should be able to help you draw up the contracts and walk you through the process. As your needs change, you can then have the attorney tweak your contracts as you see fit.

Restaurant Delivery Service

- Provide delivery services for restaurants.
- Create a small publication with menus from all the restaurants whose food you deliver and give this publication to customers who want more delivery options than pizza and Chinese food.

- Use electric, biodiesel, ethanol, or hybrid-electric vehicles for delivery purposes.
- Give prime space in your publication to restaurants serving vegetarian and/or organic food, and charge them a smaller rate than other restaurants, sort of a "green business discount."

Description

Many restaurants want to increase their potential customer base by offering delivery services, but they simply don't have enough demand to hire their own drivers. Drivers and delivery cars are expensive luxuries unless delivery is the focus of the restaurant, as is the case with pizza and Chinese food. Delivery services fill this void by making deliveries for a large number of restaurants. They also offer customers a wide variety of cuisine options, making their services attractive to both restaurants and diners.

Green It!

The most effective way to green this kind of business is to have a highly efficient delivery vehicle that can run on some sort of bio-fuel, like ethanol (E85) or biodiesel (B20, B100, or some other blend). Volkswagen TDIs (available in Jetta, Passat, or Golf) get over 40 miles per gallon, and they can use biodiesel. You might check to see what biofuels are available in your area and then purchase a vehicle that makes sense.

You will be creating some sort of basic publication that has restaurant menus in it, with your prices for delivery items labeled clearly for customers. You may choose to give away the prime space in these publications to those restaurants that serve organic and vegetarian cuisine, as an added effort to aid the green community. The prime spots will be the first menu, the last menu, the back cover, and the very middle, where the stapled binding creates a natural split. You may also wish to give discounts to green restaurants.

Getting Started

You will need to be able to create or at least oversee the creation of a menu publication. You will also want to have a Web presence that allows people to look up menus and perhaps make orders on your Web site.

Buying the right kind of vehicle will be crucial. Researching electric cars and finding out what biofuels are available in your area may help narrow your search.

The hours will be mostly midday, nights, and weekends. The major challenge, schedule and time-wise, will be your delivery time. If customers have to wait an hour for food, they will be a lot less likely to use your service again. Thus, at the bottom of each menu in your publication, indicate approximate delivery times. Consider that an order will come to you, and you will then call it in to the restaurant, who will begin preparation. If it takes the restaurant 20 minutes to make the food, then you have used up at least 30 minutes in delivery time already.

Geographic knowledge of your area and a good map or GPS system in your vehicle will help immensely in your delivery times. Limiting your delivery area to a very manageable size will prevent you from having one delivery job put the rest behind schedule.

You will also need insulated delivery cases to keep food as fresh as possible during its journey.

Finding Customers

- Direct sales
- Flyers (your menu publication)
  - Area hotels
  - Metaphysical bookstores
  - Coffee shops
  - Outdoor gear retailers

You'll need to sell your concept to restaurant owners directly. It won't be hard since you're essentially giving them free advertising and bringing them business at the same time. Distribute your publications with menus at restaurants that are in your publication, and anywhere else that has free publication distribution, like coffee shops. You should also participate actively in local blogs and look for other creative ways to reach the cyber crowd, who will be

Web savvy and therefore not need one of your publications since they can peruse your menus and order online. You will also want to decorate your delivery vehicle with clear advertising for your services, letting other drivers know what you do.

How to Charge

Delivery services make money in one of several ways. They can charge for the basic service and take a percentage of each delivery sale from the restaurants as well. They can charge nothing for restaurants to sign up and then simply add a certain percentage on to each sale to customers. They can also charge delivery customers a sliding fee that would be based on the size of the order (for example, a $10 fee for orders under $30 and $15 for orders between $31 and $60). Tips can be expected from customers.

Other Helpful Hints and Advice

A tricky question of liability arises when a customer orders some food and it shows up late, incorrect, or smelling funny. Is it your fault or the restaurant's? Make sure when you sign up a restaurant that you define this liability clearly. You could force the restaurant to assume any responsibility for reimbursing incorrect orders or foul odors and offer to split the responsibility for late deliveries.

Keep track of when your call is put in to the restaurant, and when the food is ready. If you can demonstrate that the kitchen took too long to create the food, the restaurant will be more likely to pay for the whole order. Contact your insurance agent to discuss any coverage you may need for using a personal vehicle for the job. Hire drivers with safe driving records.

Specialty Advertising

- Help businesses think outside the box with their advertising budgets.
- Use organic cotton T-shirts, recycled mugs and pencils, and other green products on which to put corporate logos.

Description

Specialty advertising is anything beyond the normal radio, TV, print, and Internet advertising that corporations do. This can include making up hats with company logos to give out at the company picnic, pens with a catchphrase printed on them, or bowling shirts for a local team, tournament, or league. The company likes this type of advertising because it gets the company's name, logo, motto, Web site, or other company information to the general public, and it does so in a way customers may appreciate, like receiving a free pen. Every time the consumers use that pen, they're seeing the company's name.

Green It!

Offer organic cotton T-shirts. Print company names on pencils made of recycled money. Put ads on the side of high-quality reusable coffee mugs. Create elegant and attractive hemp shopping bags—there's a nice broad space on each side for company information. Be creative!

Getting Started

Make sure that you can bulk order organic T-shirts, recycled toothbrushes, or whatever other product you want to sell. Contact local printing companies to get a good price on bulk printing. Make sure they can work with all the products you want to sell.

Meet with business owners or marketing agents to show them sample products. Be ready to take orders!

Finding Customers

- Direct sales
- Networking
  - Green Drinks
  - Sierra Club groups
  - Outdoors clubs

Keep a database of all existing customers, and continue to mail them catalogs once per year or as you update your merchandise, unless they specifically request that you don't. Many times, a business will simply want to reorder pens, hats, or T-shirts as they run out of them, and all you'll have to do is make it easy for them to do so, by calling them periodically and asking if they'd like to resupply.

How to Charge

Make sure you can cover your bulk purchases and your printing costs, and then add a decent margin to cover the costs of printing your catalogs and/or flyers and other expenses. Once you have a client list, this business becomes very easy because your prices are public and your customers order as they see fit.

Other Helpful Hints and Advice

There are very few insurance or legal issues to consider for this business. The usual liability insurance should be sufficient to protect you in the case of any unforeseen event.

....

Sustainability Consultant

- Be an expert in a particular field and share that expertise with others on a fee basis.
- Help others with some aspect of environmentalism in which your passion and knowledge will help them succeed in their goals.

Description

Consultants will help solve particular problems that clients may not have the time, personnel, training, or expertise to solve on their own. Consultants offer advice, oversight, and expertise.

Green It!

Take any expertise you have about some area of environmentalism, and ask yourself, "Is this information valuable to others?" If, for example, you retrofitted your own home to make it extremely energy efficient, could you convince others that you can help them do the same? If you can save them a lot of money in terms of heating, cooling, electric, and water bills, it might be very worthwhile for clients to hire you to do so. Energy consultants might conduct an energy audit and figure out where a company is wasting money and electricity.

Ecopreneurs in Action

Kevin Emerson started Wasatch Sustainability Consulting (WSC) to help businesses, governmental agencies, and nonprofits become more sustainable. His knowledge came from a thesis he wrote at the University of Edinburgh (Scotland) about making major university campuses more ecofriendly. WSC has worked with local businesses to improve their energy efficiency, product offerings, business operations, and planning processes to make them more sustainable, which in turn led to significant cost savings for these organizations.

Getting Started

This business requires the utmost experience and expertise. These qualifications "sell" you to a potential client. Learn everything you can about whatever field interests you. Hit the library and pore over books and periodicals. Do Web searches and read articles in Web archives.

You may consider first doing some pro-bono consultations for some friends who own businesses or other interested clients. This will give you experience, and you might get some trade items or services in exchange for it.

Keep records for both you and your client, and give clients attractive and well-organized print presentations with electronic backups at the end of your consulting jobs. If they have enlisted your services, they are likely to listen to you carefully, but in the long run, they will appreciate being able to look back at your recommendations again and again. They will also think of you and your company the next time they have a problem they can't solve.

Finding Customers

- Direct sales
- Web
  - www.WiseGrasshopper.com

How to Charge

You can charge as you see fit for the particular job. If you don't know how long a job will take, charging by the hour is often preferable. If you do know, you can charge by the project or by retainer, depending on the preferences of your clientele.

However you decide to charge, make sure these fees are discussed fully up front and agreed upon by all parties. Consultants can make good money. Don't be afraid to charge $200 per hour if you feel you're worth it. If you're saving your client thousands of dollars a year in electricity costs and you charge them several thousand dollars, you're essentially paying your own salary—what company wouldn't hire you?

Other Helpful Hints and Advice

Make up a contract that clarifies your duties, responsibilities, deadlines, and fees with the client. It's a good idea to have a lawyer look over this contract for anything that you've missed. The bottom line is to make sure that you get what you asked for, deliver what you've promised to deliver, and determine that everyone's satisfied. But also be sure to protect yourself legally in case something goes wrong.

Other Types of
Green Businesses

• Carbon Offsets
• Environmentally Themed E-business
• Green Venture Capitalist
• Sustainable Remodeling and Flipping Houses

Carbon Offsets

- Sell packages to consumers and businesses that allow them to offset their greenhouse gas emissions by funding "carbon sink" projects, such as reforestation.
- Invest revenues from customers' purchases in renewable energy projects.
- Give stickers and certificates to customers so they can show off their carbon neutrality, meanwhile advertising your business for free.

Description

Offsetting greenhouse gas (GHG) emissions is a relatively new field, but it has been gaining tremendous traction in recent years due to increasing evidence of global climate change and efforts such as *An Inconvenient Truth*, Al Gore's Oscar-winning documentary about global warming. Many people want to reduce their "carbon footprint" but can't afford solar panels. Buying a certificate from your company allows them to invest indirectly in projects that will offset their greenhouse gas emissions by pooling their money with other like-minded consumers for greater buying power.

Green It!

You should endeavor to "walk the walk" by going paperless in the office if possible, becoming carbon neutral yourself, and greening your office building as much as possible.

Getting Started

You'll need to contact an independent third party certifier to show that you are making your business dealings as transparent to the public as possible. Check out www.green-e.org for more details. Once you are certified to invest people's money in renewable energy and reforestation projects, you can then begin to charge people for their carbon credits, pooling the money from many customers, and investing in these projects.

You should have a background in environmental affairs and a good knowledge of renewable energy and carbon budgets. You will also need a computer, phone, Internet connection, and the ability to make sound judgments on investments. For instance, if you choose to fund a reforestation project in South America, you will want some assurance that you can then show future customers as to how many tons of greenhouse gas emissions your investment helped sequester per dollar spent.

Set up your Web site so that people can first calculate their carbon footprints and then have easy access to buying carbon credits for that amount. Calculations for the carbon footprint should include their monthly bills for heating, cooling, and electricity, the number of miles they drive, how many miles per gallon their vehicle gets, how many meat-based meals they eat, what percentage of locally grown produce and locally made goods they buy, and any other offsets they are making (like buying into their utility's renewable energy program). See www.nature.org/initiatives/climatechange/calculator for a good example.

Make sure your Web site is as transparent as possible about what kinds of investments you are making so that dubious customers will feel better about their purchases. Then make sure that customers receive a certificate on recycled paper and perhaps a sticker for their store window, house, or car. The stickers amount to free advertising for you, so make them attractive, congratulatory, and professional.

Finding Customers

- Flyers
  - Health food stores
  - Vegetarian restaurants
- Web
  - www.WiseGrasshopper.com
- Media outlets including those for niche markets
  - Local health and environmentally themed monthly magazines

Get your name out there in the green community. You can start locally, with the pooled money going to local renewable energy projects like wind farms or to local reforestation efforts. Sponsoring local events like bike races, triathlons, and sustainability shows will get your name out there and increase your client list. Once you have a customer, try to get him or her to sign up for renewals regularly.

Another avenue of finding new customers is to reach them when they are making a purchase that they might want to offset. For instance, many travel Web sites have ads for carbon-offsetting companies come up as soon as someone purchases a plane ticket. Your Web site should be able to calculate how many tons of carbon emissions the person's new purchase is going to generate, and allow for him or her to quickly offset those emissions by purchasing carbon credits from you. If you can set this sort of system up at local gas stations, car dealerships, restaurants, hotels, and so on, you might find clients at the time when they are most apt to be willing to reduce their carbon footprint.

One terrific idea, if you can find a community grocer that is willing, would be to set up a program on a grocer's checkout computer that calculates carbon emissions per item. Say, for example, that a head of broccoli produces a pound of GHGs, a gallon of milk, 10 pounds of GHGs, and a pound of red meat, 100 pounds of GHGs. The computer at the checkout could give customers the option to buy carbon offsets based on these purchases and offer them a chance to view their carbon footprint on their receipt. Their printout would then educate them on the carbon footprint of their diet (for example, the carbon footprint of a meat-based diet is much higher than a vegetarian diet). Thus, you are not only allowing them to offset their footprint but also educating them in ways that further allow them to reduce their impact. And of course, put your Web site on the receipt!

How to Charge

You will need to analyze how much it costs to offset x amount of greenhouse gas emissions. For example, if a small wind power plant that you invest in will reduce the GHGs by an equivalent of 100 cars, and the company needs you to invest $$Y$ to make its project succeed financially, you will need to charge each person who is offsetting the carbon emissions for his or her car 1/100 of the cost of that project, plus whatever overhead you have. Once you have this figure down pat, you should standardize it so that when people find out on your Web site that they are producing 7,000 pounds of greenhouse gas emissions yearly, they will know that each pound will cost 14 cents to offset, just for example.

Other Helpful Hints and Advice

Make sure you are independently certified by a third party. The other side of your business, investing in carbon-offsetting projects, will require you to research the projects independently and make sure that you're getting what you're paying for and not committing to anything unproductive or environmentally unsound.

Environmentally Themed E-business

- Create a viable Internet-based business with a focus on sustainability.
- Derive revenues from advertising, memberships, or through partnerships with green organizations that sell products or services to your members.

Description

E-business applications range in service from e-cards to e-mail, Web logs (blogs) to search engines to auctions, as well as news and information. A typical e-business provides a service to users. They can either charge for that service, directly to the user (rare) or allow the services to be used for free and sell advertising that will be viewed by users (more common).

Green It!

In an e-business, there is very little waste, little need for maintaining a brick-and-mortar building, few transportation needs, and so on. However, you can take the e-business concept as far as you would like in terms of what kind of environmental impacts you want to have.

WiseGrasshopper (www.WiseGrasshopper.com), a directory of teachers, mentors, classes, tutors, and lessons of any kind, has incorporated sustainability into its basic business model by creating a category of lessons specifically geared toward helping people live a greener lifestyle. Their green category includes lessons in sustainability topics ranging from vegetarian and vegan cooking to raw food prep, and it addresses ecocommuting training and education, organic gardeners, socially responsible investment advisors, home energy efficiency consultants, and so on.

Care2 (www.care2.com), a free Web-based e-mail service, offers its users free e-mail and storage, community networking, environmentally themed e-cards, notices of urgent environmental affairs in the political and business world, and the ability to click on links to worthy causes, where supporting advertisers donate a certain amount to those charities for every user that clicks there.

GreenMatch, LLC, produces two Web sites for green singles: www.greensingles.com and www.veggielove.com (for single vegetarians). Similarly, there is www.veggiedate.org, www. EarthwiseSingles.com, and www.EcoRoommates.com.

Red Jellyfish (www.redjellyfish.com) offers Internet service and uses part of its proceeds to prevent deforestation in the Amazon rainforest. Eco-Mall (www.Eco-Mall.com) is a clearinghouse for all things green, where you can search for anything from organic cotton athletic socks to recycled paper day planners. Green blogs exist in abundance, including TreeHugger.com, Eco-Chick.com, and IdealBite.com.

Ecopreneurs in Action

Dan Heffernan, cofounder of WiseGrasshopper (www.WiseGrasshopper.com), says that allowing "green" to be an entire category of the lessons his Web site offers brings sustainability to the attention of the users of the site, regardless of whether that person is green or not. "Someone might get on WiseGrasshopper just looking to get a guitar lesson or find a shiatsu massage class, but when they see that category "Green Your Life" at the front and center of our site, they may become introduced to aspects of sustainability they might not normally encounter elsewhere in their lives," said Heffernan. He added, "We also hope that many people who live green will make extra money teaching lessons in organic gardening, bike commuting, and so on, and therefore drive a lot more money into the green community."

Getting Started

An e-business requires some substantial investment in terms of programmers, hardware, and software, and it often requires a fair bit of maintenance throughout the life of the business. A good amount of tech-savviness would be good experience for someone looking to start an environmentally themed e-business.

You might consider this type of business if you have a background in Web design, Web graphics, advertising sales, programming, and so on, or if you have worked for other dot-com start-ups and understand the wild and wacky world of e-business.

To gain an understanding of the offerings and services of e-businesses you are interested in, check out what others are doing. If you are looking to start a blog, for example, it is a good idea to make sure that others aren't already out there doing what you want to do.

Finding Customers

- Direct sales
- Web
  - Facebook
  - Craigslist
  - Web logs (blogs)
- Press releases

If you feel overwhelmed by this aspect of the business, you might consider hiring a publicity company that specializes in environmentally conscientious businesses. These companies do much of the marketing and public relations for you, writing press releases, organizing publicity campaigns, and directing your advertising dollars to the best possible outlet.

To find advertising clients, you have a couple of options. Google and other search engines typically offer to place targeted advertisements on your website, but they take a cut of the proceeds that may be 50 to 60 percent or more, depending on your Web site's traffic. You can also go direct to the advertisers, but this method is far more labor intensive. Many start-ups find it best to let GoogleAds take care of generating some revenues for them at the beginning, and then when their site takes off and they have a lot of traffic, they are then more appealing to advertisers and can make a better pitch as a result.

How to Charge

What you charge to advertisers will largely be a result of the amount of traffic (visitors) your site gets. If your site is not entirely dependent on advertising as its sole source of revenue, you will need to figure how to charge for your other services. Mighty Bids, for example, charges sellers of products on their online auction site a percentage from each sold item.

Other Helpful Hints and Advice

Depending on the type of e-business, there will be a variety of legal and insurance issues to consider. If you are running a blog, for example, make sure you have a disclaimer stating that opinions expressed by users do not necessarily reflect those of your company.

If people are signing in as "members" on your site, you should also have a "Terms & Conditions" contract stating their rights, obligations, and duties as members, and what constitutes behavior unwelcome on your site. As these considerations will vary widely depending on the type of business, you might simply consider contacting an attorney and an insurance agent to discuss your particular needs.

Green Venture Capitalist

• Invest in emerging green businesses.

Description

Funding provided to start-up businesses by private investors is called "venture capital" (VC). A company or individual specializing in VC seeks out investment opportunities in small or start-up businesses, where the potential reward may be very good.

Venture capitalists typically receive shares (stock) in a company for the investment they make. VCs are then part owners of the company, though they usually forfeit the right (willingly) to help direct strategy or other business decisions. Thus, the investment decision is made based as much on the confidence the VC has in the entrepreneur as in the business model itself.

One way in which VCs spread out their own personal risk is to take in money from investors wishing to see a high rate of return. Individual investors may wish to invest their money with the venture capital company and let the company make investments for them. The VC, then, invests this pooled money in small or start-up companies, essentially representing their investment clients as well as themselves. If the small company does well, the VC takes a share of the money invested by individual investors and (hopefully) still gives them a substantial return on their investment.

Green It!

Seek out green businesses and provide start-up or growth money to help the company achieve short- or long-term goals. Green business is the wave of the future, and these companies, based on changing market demands and the reality of global economics (increasing population and finite resources), may well prove to be the best investments money can buy.

There are a number of Web sites that link venture capitalists to businesses seeking funding. A good one for green businesses is www.sustainablebusiness.com. You may also find good ones at the Co-op America's Web site (www.coopamerica.org) or through various business networking sites.

Getting Started

Venture capital investors need to have a surplus of free cash available to invest in companies and be able to wait a while to receive returns because there won't be much immediate return on their investments. Returns, though potentially great, may be several years away.

The other major criterion for becoming a successful VC is an intuitive sense of good business models and good businesspeople. You will find that there are many businesses looking for extra cash. Your job will be to decide which ones fit your requirements for green investing as well as which ones have the greatest potential rewards and the most solid business plans. Reserve your capital until you've heard a wide variety of pitches from entrepreneurs. As you hear more and more presentations, you will begin to understand who will make the most successful entrepreneur and which business models have the most potential. Conducting research on the side will also help you understand green businesses, emerging technologies, and their markets.

Finding Customers

- Media outlets including those for niche markets
  - Co-op America
  - National Public Radio

Customers (entrepreneurs or potential entrepreneurs) will find you fairly quickly through business networking sites or through ads you place on green business Web sites. Remember that there are more people looking for money than there are people with money to lend, so you can be fairly selective. One VC claimed that he may fund 1 out of every 400 requests he receives.

If you are running a green VC firm, you are likely to find investors who are very committed to the green movement. These folks may be as interested in the success of the green businesses as in the success of their investments. To find customers interested in this kind of investing, you might consider advertising in green publications.

How to Charge

Allow potential customers to present you with options for investment. Remember that they are trying to sell you on their business, and thus they will likely have attractive financial packages to offer you.

Your charge will most likely include partial ownership and some sort of "guaranteed buyout package" by which a company, once it starts making money, can buy back the shares of stock it issues you for your initial investment. Your charge may also include some sort of "tiered payback plan" by which the company pays you a guaranteed percentage each year plus x percent of the company's net profits. The industry standard is sometimes called the "2 and 20," meaning the company would pay the VC firm 2 percent of the invested capital and 20 percent of its net profits.

Other Helpful Hints and Advice

Make sure that any liabilities involved remain the responsibility of the entrepreneur you're working with and that the company has sufficient insurance to cover any potential lawsuits or accidents.

The business structure is also important because some business structures protect or limit owners' liabilities almost completely (limited-liability companies, S corporations, and C corporations) while others do not provide much protection (sole proprietorships and partnerships). If you have any concerns, allow a lawyer to take a look at the business documents for the company you are thinking of investing in.

Also make sure that for any people investing their money through your company, you give the basic guidelines printed at the bottom of every ad for a money management company. This fine print usually states something like, "No financial investment provides a guaranteed return on investment. You should consider the [name of the investment or investment company]'s investment objectives, risks, charges, and expenses carefully before investing." You might want to adapt something like this for your own investors, or have a lawyer craft one. Other VC firms will have similar statements, and you can get an idea of what you need to say by reading through their literature.

Sustainable Remodeling and Flipping Houses

- Work inside existing houses to update and renew interiors for the current house owners, or purchase fixer-upper houses to then remodel and sell them.
- Incorporate a variety of appropriate green building techniques and supplies for sustainable interiors, energy efficiency, and clean energy.

Description

Remodeling has a distinct advantage over new construction, and many contractors are opting to change their business model as a result. The major advantage is that the work goes on largely inside an existing structure, and therefore it evades some of the major hassles of permits, licenses, and regulations.

A remodeling company offers its services to clients looking to update their interiors. The company may remove cabinets, sinks, appliances, and walls in order to accommodate clients' desires, replacing them with newer products that are usually chosen by the consumer and perhaps in conjunction with the remodeler as well.

"Flipping" houses is a term used when remodelers buy existing homes, fix them up through remodeling, and sell them for a profit.

Green It!

You can adapt the landscaping to local conditions, tearing out Kentucky bluegrass and replacing it with a landscape of native plants, fruit trees, shade trees, and other fixtures. For ideas on remodeling the landscape, see the "Home and Office Services" entry in this book, especially the section about eco-friendly landscaping.

In the interior, you can donate usable items that you are planning to remove and replace (for example, sinks) to a local salvage yard. You can replace energy-hogging appliances with the most energy efficient ones, looking for Energy Star ratings. You can install solar hot water systems or tankless, on-demand hot water heaters (very efficient). You can install extra insulation in the attic and walls to make the house more energy efficient. Water-saving showerheads will save not only water but the energy required to heat that water. Energy-efficient lighting options will keep the house cool in the summer and save energy as well.

You can make the interior of the building healthier by using natural paints and plasters to reduce the chemical load in the house. Installing sustainable hardwood floors (FSC certified hardwoods, bamboo or cork floors) will reduce maintenance of carpeting and the dander, hair, dirt, and microbes that tend to accumulate in carpets. There are great products like Marmoleum for kitchen floors made of materials that are recycled and nontoxic.

You can also take a grander view and endeavor to support high-density housing by adding a mother-in-law apartment. This not only creates a secondary income for the owner of the house but also reduces the overall need for new housing developments by making one house effectively into two.

In working with your clients, you can offer all of these improvements and let them decide which they have the budget for. If you are flipping the house, the extent and number of improvements are up to you and your budget. In that case, make sure you keep track of all the improvements you've made, and show perspective buyers how much you're likely to save them on their heating, cooling, ventilation, water, and power bills, not to mention their home maintenance bills.

For further information and ideas about green remodeling, visit www.builditgreen.org.

Ecopreneurs in Action

Scott Dwire of PCR, a green construction and remodeling company, says, "Green construction and remodeling is just specialized knowledge of regular construction. 90 percent of what we do is standard construction techniques. I would suggest someone interested in starting in this field find someone like us, where they can learn construction *and* green techniques, then go out and start their own company. We are looking to home-grow our own subcontractors, so we would send them a lot of business. We would already know what they can do, and we would have a good working relationship with them." Dwire adds that he gets a majority of his business through referrals from the LEED certified architects in town and through the local green building supply store.

Getting Started

Consider attending a contractor's school and getting your license so that you have established credentials and a trustworthy knowledge base to draw from. Experience working for another remodeling company would also be invaluable because there are many things you cannot learn in school. Also, if you can't handle the plumbing, electrical, or any of the other necessary jobs, you will likely pay through the nose for the service of subcontractors.

Your company will need a vehicle capable of carrying large cargoes. If you can find a large diesel pickup truck, like a Ford F-350, you can use biodiesel. Check www.biodiesel.org to see if there is biodiesel available in your area.

You will also need a good array of tools and equipment. Without going into a great deal of detail, suffice it to say, a large toolbox will be required!

If you are flipping a property, you also need a chunk of capital to invest in the real estate and in the additions you'll be putting onto the house. One of the drawbacks of this business is that you don't get a paycheck throughout the process. There is only one lump sum that comes at the end. If you are prepared for this kind of strange financial schedule, there is a great deal of money to be made flipping houses—the payoff can be quite substantial in the end.

Finding Customers

- Flyers
  - Health food stores
  - Naturopathic physicians' offices
- Media outlets including those for niche markets
  - Local health and environmentally themed monthly magazines
  - Co-op America
  - National Public Radio
- Booths
  - Home and garden shows

Keep an album of photographs (before and after) of your work so you can show jobs to potential clients. Take advantage of the fact that you can produce a far healthier interior, and post flyers at natural food stores and naturopathic physicians' offices. Make sure, if you do this, that you explain that since this is a remodel, you will not be able to fully eliminate all toxins from a home but that you can replace an interior full of chemical products with a new one in which chemical paints, sealants, plasters, adhesives, and the like are not used.

If you are flipping a property, you buy the house and remodel it, and then either sell it yourself as a "for sale by owner" property or turn it over to a real estate broker who is knowledgeable in green building principles. However you sell it, make sure to promote how efficient, green, new, and low maintenance it will be.

How to Charge

If you're remodeling, you will need to submit a bid for the job. Bidding will require extensive thought on how much it will cost you to do a job, including all the materials and labor. You then need to add a fairly hefty margin to account for all the unforeseen events that may take place.

Learning how to prepare estimates and bids is another area in which your working for another company first will be beneficial.

If you're flipping a property, research the market to find out the prices of similar properties that have sold recently because the market prices may change substantially between the times you purchase the property, remodel it, and ultimately put it on the market for sale. Also, when arriving at a sales price for the property, be sure to include in the price the costs of the materials and labor that you put into the remodeling. When you are finished with the project, you will know how many hours of your labor (and that of any helpers you hire) went into the job, and you will know how much the total renovations cost. If you are turning the property over to a real estate broker who knows about green building, that person will also likely have some ideas on how to price it.

Other Helpful Hints and Advice

As with any construction site, there is a plethora of safety concerns. Hard hats, protective gloves, breathing masks, protective clothing, and other safety equipment should be the norm.

If you decide to add an apartment or other additional residence, you may have to work with zoning laws. Typically mother-in-law apartments need no approvals in terms of local zoning ordinances, but if your clients are hoping to convert what was a single-family home into an official duplex or triplex, advise them that they may have to get approval to do that from the local zoning boards.

Contracts are very important. It is recommended that you have contracts with your customers as well as with any with subcontractors, spelling out in great detail what each party's responsibilities are.

If you're flipping a property, you will want to keep the building insured during the entire process. You may also think about insuring some of the appliances, flooring products, solar panels, and other expensive add-ons against theft because the house will likely be empty. There are capital gains tax implications to this kind of business that you may want to talk to a CPA about—he or she may have some ideas on how to save some money on taxes. You will also likely be entitled to a good number of tax incentives for installing energy-efficient appliances, solar panels, and the like. Check with the IRS as well as your state revenue department, and make sure to take advantage of everything available to you. Retailers who sell the appliances, solar panels, and other energy conservation devices should also be able to help you access the tax incentives available to you.

Appendixes

- Appendix 1 Green Franchises and Other Team Opportunities
- Appendix 2 Governmental and Other Resources for Small Businesses

Green Franchises and Other Team Opportunities

This section lists green companies offering franchises or other turnkey operations, consulting services, or other business assistance to aspiring ecopreneurs looking to start businesses in their area, and the details of said offerings.

Green Carpet Cleaning

Drysdale's Carpet Cleaning Services
www.carpet-cleaning-business.com/
Contact: Mark Dullea, MarkD@cybercom.net
See pages 57–61

Lawn Mowing and Maintenance

Clean Air Lawn Care
www.CleanAirLawnCare.com
888-969-3669
See pages 72–76

Green Real Estate Brokerage

Tropisphere Realty
Santa Teresa, Costa Rica
www.tropisphere.com
See pages 100–104

Organic Food Delivery Services

Door to Door Organics
www.doortodoororganics.com
See pages 106–108

Free-Range, Organic Fresh-Mex Restaurant

Sharky's Woodfired Mexican Grill
www.sharkys.com
See pages 127–130

Organic Pizzeria

Pizza Fusion
www.pizzafusion.com
954-202-1919
See pages 136–139

Sustainable Buffet-Style Restaurant

One World Café
One World Everybody Eats Foundation
www.oneworldeverybodyeats.com
See pages 143–146

Aveda Concept Salon

Aveda
www.aveda.com
See pages 155–157

Fair Trade Retail Store

Ten Thousand Villages
www.tenthousandvillages.com/php/about.us/start.a.store.php
See pages 175–178

Printer Cartridge Refilling Store

Cartridge World
www.cartridgeworld.com
See pages 182–186

Governmental and Other Resources for Small Businesses

California Certified Organic Farmers

www.ccof.org

This nonprofit group advocates for certified organic products, through education, political advocacy, and marketing. It certifies organic agriculture, and it publishes an online organic directory.

Co-op America

www.coopamerica.org

The preeminent print and online directory of green businesses, Co-op America is a nonprofit organization dedicated to harnessing economic power for the good of the earth. This is not only a good advertising and networking outlet for your green business but also a terrific source of links and other information about running a successful green business.

Green Hotel Association

www.greenhotels.com

This group will assist you in converting your existing lodging business (including hotels, bed & breakfasts, and hostels) to a certified green lodging or in starting a new green lodging project. The organization also sells products for green lodging businesses, and it has numerous other resources for developing ecotourism projects available on its Web site.

Green Restaurant Association

www.dinegreen.com

This nonprofit organization will help in any aspect of greening the restaurant industry, including marketing, community organizing, research, consulting, and education.

Small Business Administration

www.sba.gov

The Small Business Administration (SBA) is part of the U.S. government, and it provides training, publications, and financial and other advisory services. In addition, it has programs specifically designed for minorities, veterans, and women.

www.sba.gov/sbdc

The SBA also has a division that focuses on small business development that might be helpful to someone looking to start a business. It's called the Small Business Development Centers (SBDC).

U.S. Department of Agriculture

www.usda.gov

If you are looking to work in the restaurant, catering, food delivery, or other food industry, you can obtain food safety and preparation information from the U.S. Department of Agriculture (USDA).

U.S. Department of Commerce

www.commerce.gov

The U.S. Department of Commerce (DOC) offers grants and small business opportunities catering to the government's needs for goods and/or services.

U.S. Food and Drug Administration

www.fda.gov

If you are interested in a food-based business, the U.S. Food and Drug Administration (FDA) has downloadable forms and publications regarding labeling requirements and packaging guidelines.

U.S. Department of Labor

www.dol.gov

The U.S. Department of Labor (DOL) has information about compliance issues regarding federal labor laws. Many publications are available for download on the department's Web site.

Index

Page numbers with an n indicate notes.

A

AAA (American Automobile Association), 47

AA Environmentally Safe Cleaning, 58–59

AARP (American Association of Retired People), 47

Abou-Ismail, Omar, 140

Ace Hardware, 169

Adobe software, 119

Advertising (*see* Marketing methods)

Advertising businesses, 202–204

AFM Safecoat, 58

Agriculture and farming, 76–79, 93–96, 229

Alternative transportation retail stores, 151–155

American Association of Retired People (AARP), 47

American Automobile Association (AAA), 47

American Pride, 170

Amy's Green Clean, 66

Aveda, 155–157, 228

B

Batchler, Amy, 66

Beauty products and services, 108–112, 155–157

Bed & breakfasts (B&Bs), 8, 43–47

Benedict, Thom, 176–177

Bennett, Steven J., 3n, 10

Benson, Tom, 29

Better World Club (BWC), 47

Bianchi bikes, 159

Bike shops, 6–7, 151–155, 157–161

Biodiesel fuel, 64, 75, 87–90, 104, 166, 220

Biria bikes, 159

Black and Decker, 72–74

Blogs, 19, 116, 201–202, 211–214

Book stores, 186–189

Brandt, Ian, 147–148

Breezer bikes, 159

Broadway bikes, 159

Buffet-style restaurants, 143–146

Building supply stores, 169–175

Burt's Bees, 7–8

Business ideas (*See* Green
   businesses; *specific
   businesses, e.g.*, restaurants
   and cafés)
Butte Creek beer, 136

C

Caddell, Wesley, 88
Cairncross, Frances, 3n
California Certified Organic
   Farmers, 229
Cannondale bikes, 159
Carbon offsets, 207–210
Care2, 211–212
Carpet and floor cleaning, 57–61
Cartridge World, 183–184, 186,
   228
Catering services, 49–51
Central Book Exchange, 187
Cerreta, Denise, 144
Chlorine, 65–66, 82–83, 109
Chouinard, Yvon, 17
Clean Air Lawn Care, 73–74,
   76, 227
Clean and Green Rentals, 41
Cleaning products and methods,
   7–8, 28, 30–32, 33, 58–59,
   65–68
Cleaning services, 5–6, 65–68
Clorox, 7–8
Cockerillé, Maryann, 110
Coffee and coffee shops, 11–12,
   130–133, 134, 188
Community-supported organic
   agriculture, 93–96
The Complete Book of Raw Food
   (Baird & Rodwell), 140
Consignment stores, 161–165

Cool Cleaning Technologies, 32
Co-op America, 19, 54, 111,
   215, 229
Council, Van, 156
Craigslist, 16
Customer sources, 14

D

Day spas, 108–112
Delivery and distribution services
   biodiesel fuel, 87–90
   edible "floral" arrangements,
      165–169
   food shopping and delivery,
      106–108
   pizzerias, 136–139
   publication distribution, 9–11,
      121–125
   restaurant delivery, 199–202
Department of Agriculture
   (USDA), 230
Department of Commerce
   (DOC), 230
Department of Energy (DOE),
   192
Department of Labor (DOL),
   231
Diet planning and fitness
   training, 97–100
Dodge, 7
Door to Door Organics, 108, 228
Drinking Liberally, 16
Dry cleaning services, 30–33
Drysdale's All Natural Carpet
   Care, 59, 61, 227
Dullea, Mark, 59, 61
Dwire, Scott, 220
Dynamic bikes, 159

E

E, the Environmental Magazine, 113, 116

Earth Goods General Store, 176–177

EarthSave, 16

E-businesses, 211–214

EcoBroker certification, 101

The Eco-Foods Guide (Barstow), 147

Eco-Mall, 212

Eco-Moto, 152–153

EcoTimber, 170, 197

Ecotourism (*see* Tourism and related services)

Edible and organic "floral" arrangements, 165–169

The Elements of Organic Gardening (HRH The Prince of Wales and Donaldson), 95

Emerson, Kevin, 205

Eminence Organics, 109

Entertainment and events planning, 49–55

Environmental Home Center, 63

Environmentally-themed E-businesses, 211–214

Environmental Protection Agency (EPA), 30–31, 72, 192

Event planning, 49–51

The Exchange, 162–163

F

Facebook, 16

Fair Trade products and stores, 11–12, 130–132, 175–176

Family considerations, 12

Farming and agriculture, 76–79, 93–96, 229

Fitness training and diet planning, 97–100

Floor cleaning, 57–61

Floor products and installation, 62–65, 170, 219

Floral arrangements, 165–169

Flyers, 15–16

Food and Drug Administration (FDA), 230–231

Food products and services (*see also* Organic foods; Restaurants and cafés)
catering, 49–51
community-supported agriculture, 93–96
food shopping and delivery, 106–108
gift baskets, 90–93
health food stores, 15–16, 92, 142, 168
restaurant delivery, 199–202
wedding and event planning, 51–55

Forest Stewardship Council (FSC), 62–63, 171

Franchise opportunities (*see* Team opportunities)

Freelance writing, 115–117

Free-range meats, 127–130

"Fresh Mex" cuisine, 127–130

Fuel-efficient transportation, 7, 36, 40–41, 81, 107, 122, 200, 220

Fundraisers and grant writers, 191–193

G

Gardening and horticulture
   community-supported
      agriculture, 93–96
   landscape design, 68–71
   lawn mowing and landscape
      maintenance, 72–76
   native and organic plant
      nurseries, 179–182
   organic garden creation, 76–79
Giant bikes, 159
Giard, Kelly, 73–74
Gift basket service, 90–93
Gordon, Michael, 137
Gore, Al, 207
Government agency resources,
   114, 192, 230–231
Grant writers and fundraisers,
   191–193
Green Building Center, 171–172
Green businesses (*see also* Team
   opportunities; *specific
   business, e.g.*, personal
   services)
   customer sources, 14
   defined, 4–7
   finding the right business,
      7–13
   as green consumers, 20–21
   ideas for, 23–26
   marketing methods, 13–20
   pricing, 24–25
   resources, 32, 114, 192,
      229–231
   rules for, 8–13
   sustainability, 1–7
Green Drinks, 16

Green Earth Cleaning, 31–32, 33
Green Hotel Association, 45, 52,
   111, 113, 229
Greenhouse Bed & Breakfast, 45
Greenhouse gas (GHG) offsets,
   207–210
GreenMatch LLC, 212
Green Pages, 19, 54
Greenpeace, 31
Green product catalogs, 117–121
Green product retail stores,
   175–178
Green Restaurant Association,
   230
Grow Wild Nursery, 180
Guia (B&B owner), 45
Guilt trap, 10–11

H

Haggerty, James, 94
Hair and skin care products,
   108–112, 155–157
Hawken, Paul, 2n
Health2Go!, 98–99
Health food stores, 15–16, 92,
   142, 168
Heffernan, Dan, 212
Heron bikes, 159
Hina Adventures, 37
Home cleaning services, 5–6,
   65–68 (*see also* House and
   office services)
Home Depot, 169–170
Hopkins, Uluwehi, 37
Hotels, 43–47, 52, 111–113,
   229
Hot tubs, 82–85, 109

House and office services
    carpet and floor cleaning, 57–61
    cleaning products, 7–8, 28,
        30–32, 33, 58–59, 65–68
    cleaning services, 5–6, 65–68
    floor installation, 62–65, 170,
        219
    landscape design, 68–71
    lawn mowing and landscape
        maintenance, 72–76
    organic garden creation and
        maintenance, 76–79
    painting, 15, 79–81, 170
    pool and spa cleaning and
        maintenance, 82–85
    remodeling and flipping
        houses, 218–223
hydrogen peroxide, 83

I
Incline bikes, 159
An Inconvenient Truth (Gore),
    207
Independent publicists, 194–196
Independent sales
    representatives, 11–12,
    196–199
Industrial Supply, 169
Inn Serendipity, 45
Insurance (see specific businesses)
Internet (see also Web sites)
    blogs, 19, 116, 201–202,
        211–214
    E-businesses, 211–214
    marketing on, 16, 19–20,
        213–214
Irrigation systems, 76–78

J
Jordan, Ben, 88
Juice and smoothie bars, 133–136

K
Kona bikes, 159

L
Landscape creation and
        maintenance
    design services, 68–71
    lawn mowing and yard
        maintenance, 72–76
    organic gardens, 76–79
Laundromats, 27–30
Lazar, Vaughn, 137
Leave No Trace principles, 36
LEED (Leadership in Energy
        Efficiency and Design)
        certification, 4
Let My People Go Surfing
        (Chouinard), 17
Licenses and permits (see specific
        businesses)
Liquefied carbon dioxide,
        31–32, 33
Living Cuisine, 140
Living in the Raw (Calabro),
        141
Loan sources, 32
Local Harvest, 93, 95
LOHAS (lifestyle of health and
        sustainability) consumers, 3,
        20–21, 101, 167
Lovins, Armory, 2n
Lovins, Hunter, 2n
Lowe's, 169–170

Lowe, Scott, 176
Lynch, Meg, 131–132

M
Magretta, Joan, 2n
Manufacturing and wholesale
    production
  biodiesel cooperatives, 87–90
  community-supported
    agriculture, 93–96
  gift basket service, 90–93
Marine Stewardship Council
    (MSC), 4, 128
Mark (B&B owner), 45
Marketing methods
  challenges, 13–14
  customer sources, 14
  delivery vehicle signage, 123,
    138, 202
  flyers, 15–16
  Internet, 16, 213–214
  location, 14–15
  media outlets, 19–20, 177
  networking, 16–17, 173
  press releases, 17–19
  teaching classes, 142, 173–174
Marmoleum, 63, 219
Marsh, Casey, 162–163
McCabe, Geoff, 102
McLaughlin, Deanna, 98–99
Media (see Marketing methods)
Miele, 32
Mighty Bids, 214

N
National Public Radio (NPR),
    19, 177
Native plant nurseries, 179–182

Networking, 16–17, 173
New Belgium beer, 136
Niche-market media outlets,
    19–20
Nonprofit organizations (see
    Services to businesses and
    nonprofit organizations)
North, Jay, 95

O
Office cleaning services, 5–6,
    65–68
Offsetting greenhouse gas (GHG)
    emissions, 207–210
One World Café, 144–145, 228
One World Everybody Eats
    (OWEE) Foundation, 144,
    146, 228
Organic Consumers Association,
    166
Organic foods (see also
    Restaurants and cafés)
  agriculture and farming,
    76–79, 93–96, 229
  catering and events, 49–53
  coffee, 11–12, 130–133, 134,
    188
  defined, 130
  delivery services for,
    106–108
  diet planning with, 97–100
  edible "floral" arrangements,
    165–169
  in gift baskets, 91
Organic gardens or farms, 76–79,
    93–96, 179–182, 229 (see
    also Landscape creation and
    maintenance)

P

Painting products and services, 15, 79–81, 170
Patagonia, 6, 17–18
Patterson, Ashley, 171–172
PCR, 220
Peace Corps, 114
Pedersen, Pam, 187
Peoples' Fuel Cooperative, 88
Perchloroethylene (perc), 30–31
Permaculture Credit Union, 32
Permits and licenses *(see specific businesses)*
Personal services
  day spas, 108–112
  fitness training and diet planning, 97–100
  real estate brokerage, 100–104
  restaurant or grocery delivery, 106–108, 199–202
  shuttle services, 104–106
  travel planning, 112–114
Personal sustainability project (PSP), 4
Pizza Fusion, 137, 139, 228
Pizzerias, 136–139
Plant nurseries, 179–182
Polycube Media, 122
Polyurethane, 58
Pool and spa cleaning and maintenance, 82–85
Pricing of products and services, 24–25 *(see also specific businesses)*
Printer cartridge refilling stores, 182–186
Product catalog producers, 12, 117–121

Product retail stores, 175–178
Publicists, 194–196
Publishing and related businesses
  freelance writers, 115–117
  product catalog producers, 12, 117–121
  publication distribution services, 121–125

Q

Quark software, 119

R

Raw food bars, 139–143
Real estate brokerage, 100–104
Rechelbacher, Horst, 156
Recycled or reused products, 2, 6, 182–189 *(see also specific businesses)*
Red Jellyfish, 212
Reinhardt, Forest, 2n
Remodeling and flipping houses, 218–223
Rental operations, 40–43, 53
Restaurants and cafés
  bed and breakfasts, 44–45
  buffet-style, 143–146
  coffee shops, 130–133, 188
  delivery services for, 199–202
  fresh-Mex, 127–130
  juice and smoothie bars, 133–136
  pizzerias, 136–139
  raw food bars, 139–143
  vegan, 146–149
Retail food and food services *(see Food products and services; Restaurants and cafés)*

Retail nonfood operations
  alternative transportation
    retail stores, 151–155
  Aveda concept salons, 155–157
  bike shops, 6–7, 151–155,
    157–161
  building supply stores,
    169–175
  consignment stores, 161–165
  edible "floral" arrangements,
    165–169
  green product stores, 175–178
  native and organic plant
    nurseries, 179–182
  printer cartridge refilling
    stores, 182–186
  used-book exchanges, 186–189
Revolution Cuisine (Brandt), 148
Rivendell bikes, 159
Rodale's Illustrated Encyclopedia
  of Organic Gardening
  (Kruger), 95
Rules for ecopreneurs, 8–13

S
Sage's Café, 147–148
Sales representatives, 11–12,
  196–199
Saturday Cycles, 159
Schaerer, Jennifer, 183–184
Schlee, Jon, 153
Services to businesses and
    nonprofit organizations (see
    also Delivery and
    distribution services; Food
    products and services;
    House and office services;
    Personal services; Tourism
    and related services)
  fundraisers and grant writers,
    191–193
  independent publicists,
    194–196
  independent sales
    representatives, 11–12,
    196–199
  restaurant delivery services,
    199–202
  specialty advertising, 202–204
  sustainability consultants,
    204–206
Seventh Generation, 28
Shapiro, Robert, 2n
Sharky's Mexican Grill, 130, 228
ShoreBank Pacific, 32
Shuttle services, 104–106
Sierra Club, 8, 16–17
Skin care products, 111, 155–157
Small Business Administration
  (SBA), 230
Small Business Development
  Centers (SBDC), 230
Smoothie bars, 133–136
Soma bikes, 159
Specialized bikes, 159
Specialty advertising, 202–204
Sprinter vans, 81, 107, 122
Sroat, Ena, 37
Standard Builders, 169
Stone Mill beer, 136
Straus Communications, 195
Straus Family Creamery, 195
Straus, Michael, 195
Success and guilt, 9–11
Sunday, Mark, 159
Sun River Farms, 94
Surly bikes, 159
Sustainability, 1–7

Sustainability consultants, 204–206
Sustainable Forest Initiative (SFI), 63, 171

T
Team opportunities
  about, 25
  house and office services, 61, 76
  personal services, 103, 108
  retail food and food services, 130, 139, 146
  retail nonfood operations, 178, 186
  summary, 227–228
Ten Thousand Villages, 176, 178, 228
TerraPass, 53
Tourism and related services
  bed & breakfasts, 43–47
  tour operators, 35–40
  transport rental operations, 40–43, 53
  travel planning, 112–114
Transportation
  bike shops, 6–7, 151–155, 157–161
  biodiesel cooperatives, 87–90
  biodiesel fuel sources, 64, 75, 104, 166, 220
  fuel-efficient, 7, 36, 40–41, 81, 107, 122, 200, 220
  rental operations, 40–43, 53
  retail stores, 151–155
  shuttle services, 104–106
Trek bikes, 159
Triple-certified coffee, 11–12, 130–131, 134, 188
Tropisphere Realty, 102, 103, 227

U
University of Edinburgh (Scotland), 205
U.S. government agency resources, 114, 192, 230–231
U.S. Green Building Council (USGBC), 4n, 102, 170, 172
Used-book exchanges, 186–189

V
Van Michael Salon, 156
Vegan food and cafés, 140, 146–149, 211
Vegetarian food
  bed and breakfast meals, 44–45
  carbon offsets and, 210
  diet planning and, 98
  E-business and, 211–212
  at events, 52
  marketing opportunities, 15–16
  restaurants and cafés, 130–132, 134, 139–143, 147–148
Velo Rouge Café, 131–132
Venture capitalists, 214–217
Viral Web marketing, 16
Volatile organic compounds (VOCs), 15, 31, 58, 62–63, 72, 79–80
Volkswagen TDIs, 200

W
Walley, Noah, 2n
Wal-Mart, 4
Wasatch Sustainability Consulting (WSC), 205
Waterlox, 58

Web sites *(see also* Internet;
  specific company names)
AhhNatural.com, 82–83
BelloMundo.com, 113
biodieselamerica.org, 89
bluebottlecoffee.net, 130
BodyAndSoulRetreat.com, 110
builditgreen.org, 219
caffeibis.com, 130, 197
cleanairgardening.com, 78
EarthwiseSingles.com, 212
Eco-Chick.com, 212
ecoparti.com, 53
EcoRoommates.com, 212
EcoTour.org, 113
enn.com, 116
Expedia.com, 53
goingorganic.com, 95
green-e.org, 208
greensingles.com, 212
grist.org, 116
IdealBite.com, 212
nature.org, 208

organicbouquet.com, 53
organicvintners.com, 52
ozocar.com, 53
responsibletravel.com, 113
sustainablebusiness.com, 215
SustainableTravel.com, 113
SustainableTravelInternational.
  org, 113
TreeHugger.com, 212
tryvegetarian.org, 147
vegan.org, 147
vegcooking.com, 148
veggiedate.com, 212
veggielove.com, 212
wetcleaning.com, 31
Wedding and event planners,
  51–55
Wells Fargo, 4–5
Weyher, Gayle, 180
Whitehead, Bradley, 2n
Whole Foods Market, 7
WiseGrasshopper, 16, 211–212
Writing, freelance, 115–117

About the Author

Scott Cooney is a serial ecopreneur who has started, grown, and sold multiple green businesses. He has also consulted others on starting their own green business. A tireless champion of sustainability, Cooney cofounded and published a green business directory for the greater Salt Lake City area, and he has written for numerous publications on business and social responsibility. He currently serves as a project manager for the global sustainability consulting firm Saatchi & Saatchi S in beautiful San Francisco, California.